The Wines of
New Mexico

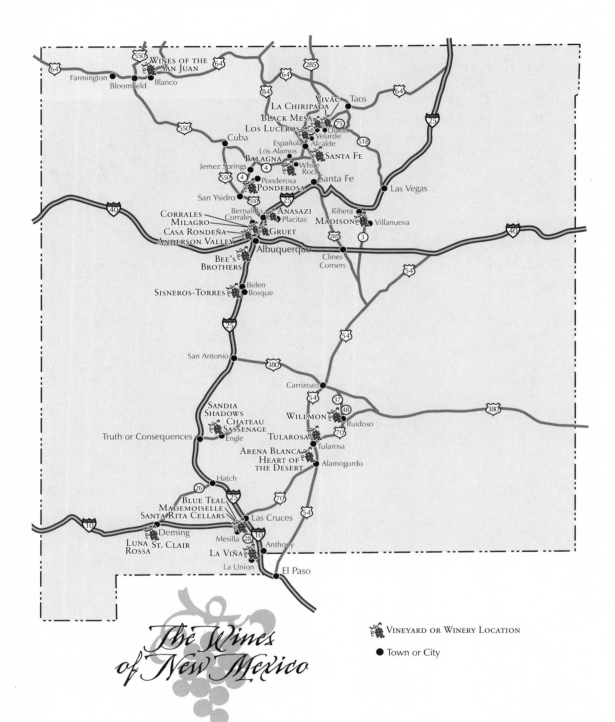

WINES OF THE
SAN JUAN
550
Farmington
64
64
Bloomfield Blanco
285
64
84
VIVÁC Taos
LA CHIRIPADA
64
BLACK MESA Dixon
LOS LUCEROS 68 Velarde
Cuba Española Alcalde 518
550 Los Alamos
BALAGNA Santa Fe
Jemez Springs 4 White SANTA FE
550 4 Rock
Ponderosa Santa Fe
PONDEROSA
San Ysidro 25 Las Vegas
550 ANASAZI
Bernalillo Placitas Ribera
CORRALES Corrales MADISON Villanueva
MILAGRO GRUET 285
CASA RONDEÑA 3
ANDERSON VALLEY Albuquerque 40
Clines
BEE'S Corners
BROTHERS 54
Belen
SISNEROS-TORRES Bosque
25
54
San Antonio
380
Carrizozo
54 37
SANDIA 48
SHADOWS WILLMON
CHATEAU Ruidoso
SASSENAGE 70
Truth or Consequences Engle TULAROSA
Tularosa
ARENA BLANCA
HEART OF
THE DESERT Alamogordo
Hatch
26
BLUE TEAL 25
MADEMOISELLE 70
SANTA RITA CELLARS Las Cruces
10 54
Deming
LUNA ST. CLAIR Mesilla 28 Anthony
ROSSA 10
LA VIÑA
La Union
El Paso

*The Wines
of New Mexico*

🍇 VINEYARD OR WINERY LOCATION
● Town or City

The Wines of New Mexico

ANDY
SANDERSIER

UNIVERSITY OF NEW MEXICO PRESS   ALBUQUERQUE

YEAR   PRINTING
11 10 09 08 07 06 05   1   2   3   4   5   6   7

LIBRARY OF CONGRESS CATALOGING-IN-PUBLICATION DATA

Sandersier, Andy, 1918–
   The wines of New Mexico / Andy Sandersier.
        p. cm.
   Includes indexes.
   ISBN 0-8263-3252-8 (pbk. : alk. paper)
   1. Wineries—New Mexico—Guidebooks.
   2. Wine and wine making—New Mexico—Guidebooks.
   3. New Mexico—Guidebooks. I. Title.
       TP557.S226 2005
       641.2'2'09789—dc22

                              2005007879

All photographs are by Andy Sandersier
unless otherwise indicated.

Maps ©2005 University of New Mexico Press
created by Kathleen Sparkes

Book design and composition Kathleen Sparkes
Body type is Sabon 10/14
Display type is Serlio and Arcana Manuscript

Although the author and publisher have
made every effort to provide accurate,
up-to-date information, they accept
no responsibility for loss, injury, or
inconvenience sustained by any person
using this book.

CONTENTS

Appendices

Indices

Foreword

The first wine festival was held in Bernalillo in 1988, while I was president of the New Mexico Vine and Wine Society. Labor Day weekend was selected for this event, and it was a success from the start. This achievement encouraged the group to have a wine festival in southern New Mexico, selecting Mesilla as the location and Memorial Day weekend as the date. These two festivals, now coupled with respective fall festivals and another one in Santa Fe, have helped wine producers enormously to sell their wines, especially small wineries with no budget for advertising.

In the last decade there have been some problems with New Mexico wineries—financial and otherwise. Most large European wineries or vineyards disappeared; others have come and gone (despite success in the wine quality and the selling) mainly for personal reasons. But those that are still in the wine-producing business are manufacturing it with style, making wine quality their utmost important issue. Indeed, the quality of New Mexico wines can be compared with similar wines in California or Europe, and they have their medals to prove it. Besides superb varietal wines there are also outstanding blended wines that command high prices (some of them with limited supply). This is true even though some wine connoisseurs said wines from French hybrid grapes would never have the quality asked for by the consumer.

Having witnessed the beginning of the wine industry in New Mexico, and being overwhelmed by its success, it gives me real pleasure to introduce Andy Sandersier's book, *The Wines of New Mexico*. It fills a gap that needed to be filled. Even though the New Mexico Vine and Wine Society (and the new organization, the New Mexico Wine Growers Association) has published several maps with the names of wineries and directions, this book is taking us to a different level, including lots of information needed for wine lovers to visit New Mexico wineries.

The book is not only easy to read, but also describes accurately both the wineries and their wine, which is always advantageous when you are looking for a particular wine or blend. Andy has followed the pattern of his other books—a downright simple approach toward a given subject (wines in this case), covering all the bases in a straightforward manner that's easy to follow and understand.

Congratulations, Andy, no doubt your book will be a smash hit.

Esteban A. Herrera, PhD, Professor Emeritus
Former NMSU Extension Horticulturist

Preface

In the months of planning this book, and during the personal visits to each area included in the project, I was determined to keep this guide simple and straightforward and not let nonessential facts clutter and defeat its intent to be a guide: a simple, concise account containing information and directions for the traveler. Now and again I allowed some important history of interest to seep into the narrative, but I've tried diligently to let brevity be my guide.

The primary purpose of this book is threefold:

1. To provide a rapid method for the user to pinpoint the location of a winery and its vicinity.

2. To show its proximity to New Mexico's largest and most populated city, Albuquerque, and its approximate distance from a few major cities bordering the state, and also to acquaint the reader with the particular area's facilities and privileges.

3. Above all, its purpose is to introduce the novice to the wine industry and its history in a simplified account—the types of grapes used to produce table wines, sparkling wines, and white wines; a brief history of wine production and its proper service, use in cooking, and proper storage; and its appreciation when consumed with meals and in moderation. In essence, this book is intended to explore and to simplify the seemingly complex and vast subject of oenology (the study of wine). Once the veil is lifted, the subject becomes clear and the sense of adventure of tasting and evaluating the many wines enhances one's appreciation of wine. The more you learn, the more your appreciation. Even the best connoisseurs admit that they never stop learning.

The book is sectioned into three zones (see the map of the entire state on page xvi). An overview map of each zone and a list of the wineries located in that zone precedes each section of this guide.

An appendix section is devoted to brief informational guides to the most asked questions about wine, i.e., proper storage, cooking with wine, service, etc. (see page 110). For quick referral, the index lists wineries and each one's zone, and the nearest town or village (see page 124).

It is my hope to tell something of the long story about the past for the area in which we live. It is hoped, too, that one of the most fascinating periods of New Mexico's history has been revealed and better understood, and the reasons for the wine industry's growth here more fully appreciated. If the interest of the readers of this book is stimulated and an intelligent curiosity is aroused, then the real purpose of this book will have been achieved.

—A. S.

Acknowledgments

There are many people that I wish to thank for providing their time and assistance while I was collecting materials for this book. First, I wish to acknowledge and give a special thanks to David Holtby, editor at the University of New Mexico Press, who seemingly was impressed by an old publication of *A Guide to the Wines of Bordeaux*, which I had produced years ago. Mr. David Holtby suggested to my editor at that time, Durwood Ball, that I produce a book on the wines of New Mexico. After just completing the book *The Lakes of New Mexico* with the help of my editor Durwood Ball and the professional staff of University of New Mexico Press, I welcomed this new opportunity and challenge to compile a guide to one of my passions, *wine*—its mystique, its history, and its romance.

My knowledge of some of the wines of Europe was indeed helpful in providing a foundation for writing about New Mexico wines, since the varietals used in France, Germany, and Italy bear the same names and these names have been adapted to those grown here in New Mexico, so I kept a diary of each winery and vineyard that I visited. This book is a compilation of notes, observations, photographs, hand-drawn maps, and research made on personal visits to each winery and its vicinity. Interviews with owners or personnel of the wineries are featured in this book. Certain historical facts in the narratives, roadside markers, and the above-mentioned interviews and conversations were verified through extensive reading of New Mexico history. With the exception of the Los Luceros Winery photograph sent to me by Bruce Noel and the beautiful photograph of the entrance to the Wines of the San Juan Tasting Room in Blanco, New Mexico, provided to me by Marcia Arnold (and for which I am very grateful), the preparation of this book has, from beginning to end, been a one-man project. I employed no researchers, photographers, or cartographers.

I am indebted to my friend and Mayor of Corrales, New Mexico, Gary Kanin, who contributed generously of his time and provided information on Corrales and its contribution to the wine industry. I am grateful to numerous others whose unselfish cooperation improved my own efforts. To Claudia Chittim, Executive Director of the New Mexico Wine Growers Association, who provided invaluable, updated information on the wineries of New Mexico. To Roberta Widner, who interrupted her duties at New Mexico State University to provide the needed guidance and transportation to the La Union, Mesilla, and Las Cruces vineyards and tasting rooms, and who provided me with some important historical facts about the region. I owe a special thanks to Dr. Esteban Herrera, Professor Emeritus and horticulturist of New Mexico State University, Las Cruces, who shared his wealth of knowledge regarding the New Mexico wine industry, and who read the manuscript and provided the Foreword for this book. Many thanks to Royce and Roz Russell, whose tour and contribution of their firsthand knowledge of the Ruidoso area was indeed helpful. I also owe a fond *thank you* to my good friends Loré and

Van White, who generously offered to guide me to the high northern country vineyards, an offer that I gratefully accepted, and who proved that the art of wine tasting is more pleasurably enjoyed in the presence of good company. To Jim Fish of the Anasazi Fields Winery, who was always available to answer some of my many questions, and to UNM Press editorial assistants Lisa Pacheco and Lincoln Bramwell, and book designer, Kathleen Sparkes, whose helpful guidance through this book's design and final preparation made its publication possible.

Finally, I am especially indebted to the many proprietors and staff of the wineries, who responded to my requests for information and who have given me the benefit of their knowledge, and some of whom went to the trouble of sending me detailed, well-considered memoranda from which I derived great profit. I also owe my deep thanks to Maureen Wynne of Casa Rondeña Winery, whose contribution to the Casa Rondeña story was greatly appreciated. Lastly, I owe a great deal to television investigative reporter Larry Barker, who made me feel incredibly fortunate to have his assistance in guiding me through the technical hurdles of the final electronic processing of the script for presentation to my publisher. To all of the above and to others too numerous to mention, I feel a great indebtedness.

—*A. S.*

xiv

Introduction

The culture of grapes can be traced back to Asia Minor between 6000 and 4000 B.C. As chronicled in both the Old and the New Testaments, wine was used to celebrate the Hebrew Sabbath and the Eucharist in the Christian Mass. Wine has been known for thousands of years in all Mediterranean countries. The Roman legions planted vineyards as they invaded as far north as the Rhine and east to the Danube. Wherever they went the Roman victors planted their vines. The crusaders planted cuttings in Europe that they brought back from the Middle East. The Vikings told of huge vines heavily festooned with grapes on this new continent that they were exploring. They called it Vineland. At the beginning of the first century B.C. the culture of the vine was developed in Gaul (Marseille). The vintners of Marseille became masters of viticulture. They knew the art of pruning, which is so necessary to the quantity and quality of the yield. During the first century B.C., they even invented and developed weather-resistant vines.

By the end of the first century they exported wine over the entire known world. In the seventeenth century the Spaniards traveled from Mexico up the west coast of California and planted at each mission, supplying wine for the Sacraments and to welcome the thirsty travelers who followed. Then in 1848 the gold rush began after gold was discovered on Sutter's Field, the property owned by John Sutter. In the words of an authority of the times, it created the greatest migration since the Crusades in the lust for gold. It was then that wine had its notable beginning in California, when in 1857 Agoston Haraszthy, a Hungarian, was not after gold, but land to plant his vines. He planted one thousand cuttings that he brought from Europe to Buena Vista in Sonoma, California, crediting him with the title of "the Father of California viticulture," but long before the coming of Agoston Haraszthy, the vines of New Mexico were thriving. They had their beginning when Spaniards from Mexico, then known as New Spain, led a group of colonists north into New Mexico.

In 1598, when Don Juan de Oñate's expedition arrived from the south through the dangerous and forbidding desert known as *La Jornada del Muerto* (Journey of the Dead Man), the weary travelers, some of them ill and starving, camped on the east bank of the Rio Grande. The friendly, century-old pueblo of Pilabo Piro Indians who inhabited the area gave them much-needed food, grain, and other supplies. Accompanying Oñate on the expedition were two Franciscan priests who remained to do missionary work among the Indians. The priests named the village *Nuestra Señora del Perpetuo Socorro* (Our Lady of Perpetual Help). It later became Socorro, in gratitude and recognition of the help that they had received from the Indians.

As was the custom, the Franciscan priests who accompanied expeditions planted vines so that they could make the wine that was needed to celebrate the Eucharist (symbolizing the Blood of Christ) in the Catholic mass. The vines were planted at or near the missions that they established. The vines produced Mission grapes, as they were called. In 1615, the priests, with the help of the

I

Indians, built the San Miguel village, completing it in 1626. At that time, in order to protect the interests of the grape growers in Spain, who derived revenues from sales of wine to the colonists, the Spanish established a law that prohibited the growing of grape-producing vines in the New World.

This control put an extreme burden on the colonists due to the high costs and long delays in shipments by oxcart from Veracruz in southeastern Mexico. In order to continue their traditional celebration of the Eucharist in their mass, the Franciscan priests, with the approval of the territorial governor, defied and ignored the control law. In 1629 they planted the first vineyards at Seneca, a Piro Indian pueblo south of Socorro and just north of the present small village of San Antonio, establishing New Mexico as the oldest winemaking region in the country.

Gradually, the plantings of vines spread throughout the region of the Rio Grande to the Mesilla Valley, an area just north of Las Cruces where most of the vineyards thrive in the deeply stratified, well-drained alluvial soil, an ideal condition for growing grapes. The spread continued on along the Rio Grande from San Antonio to Albuquerque, which later became the winemaking capital of New Mexico. Vineyards also spread through the Mimbres Valley, an area of the Mimbres River from north of Mimbres to south of Columbus. The conditions for viticulture were ideal in these areas. Climate, soil, and altitude have an enormous influence on the final attributes and character of the wine from which the grapes are grown. Sites near a river with stony soils are influenced by the nearness of the water, but also profit by being near the hills where rocks and stone walls store heat from the sun. (The practice of using stones for heat storage is still practiced in some of the vineyards of France, where vintners stack quartz rocks beneath the vines to reflect the sun.) Vines need a temperate climate. They cannot survive harsh cold or heat. New Mexico meets all of the requirements for good grape production. At an altitude that ranges between 4,800 and 5,000 feet, the climate of low rainfall, hot summers, and long cool nights is ideal.

Nevertheless, the rapid spread of vines was short-lived. About forty years later, in 1675, Apaches attacked Seneca, killing all the missionaries and many of the villagers. Those who survived fled to Isleta, Socorro, and other pueblos. Then in 1680 a well-planned revolt led by the Indian leader Popé drove the colonists out. The survivors fled to El Paso. The Apaches controlled the area until 1692 when Don Diego de Vargas established Spanish control over the territory. In 1816 the Spanish crown awarded twenty-one families a land grant. Five years later the abandoned San Miguel Mission was rebuilt on its original site and wine production resumed, igniting another surge of vine cultivation and winemaking. After 1846, New Mexico became a part of the United States and Archbishop Lamy, a French-born priest and then head of the Catholic Church in the territory, invited Italian Jesuits to Albuquerque. They planted cuttings in Old Town, Albuquerque, and were followed by French vintners, who created another explosion of wine production. Farmers throughout the region around Albuquerque devoted much of their acreage to grape cultivation and more and more wineries opened throughout the region. A great influx of vintners from Europe immigrated to the area, bringing with them their winemaking skills. After the turn of the century this prosperity took a distressing turn when unfavorable weather, floods, and freezes damaged vineyards along the entire Rio Grande from El Paso to Bernalillo. The problems were compounded by the passing of Prohibition, which made wine production illegal.

2

Prohibition was a disaster for the wine industry. After its repeal in 1934, New Mexico wineries were reopened, but met with strong competition from California wineries. These wineries produced vast quantities of wine at cheaper prices for consumers, making it impossible for New Mexican vintners to be competitive, so New Mexico wineries dwindled in size and number.

In the 1980s, the staggering California land costs attracted European vintners and investors to the less expensive New Mexico land. Consortiums of French winemakers, investors, and grape growers moved in, purchased land, and planted thousands of acres north and west of Las Cruces, reaching from the Mimbres Valley to Deming, south to Columbus, south to Lordsburg, and north from Albuquerque to Dixon.

The wine industry in New Mexico is now reversing its decline. Due to the knowledge and skills of the newly transplanted European vintners, their wines can stand taste and quality comparisons with not only the finer wines of California, but even with those of the higher-priced imports from France, Germany, and Italy.

It is fitting now that we salute these people, the growers and the winemakers who practice the art of winemaking and those who have invested and risked failure in their venture into grape production. Each cask, each bottle of wine, tells a tale of years of struggle—from facing the risks subject to the hazards of weather and diseases that threaten their crops to fluctuating prices and high labor costs—yet through their dedication we are now witnessing the fulfillment of some of their dreams.

Now, in the following pages, let us meet some of these stars of the New Mexico wine industry.

3

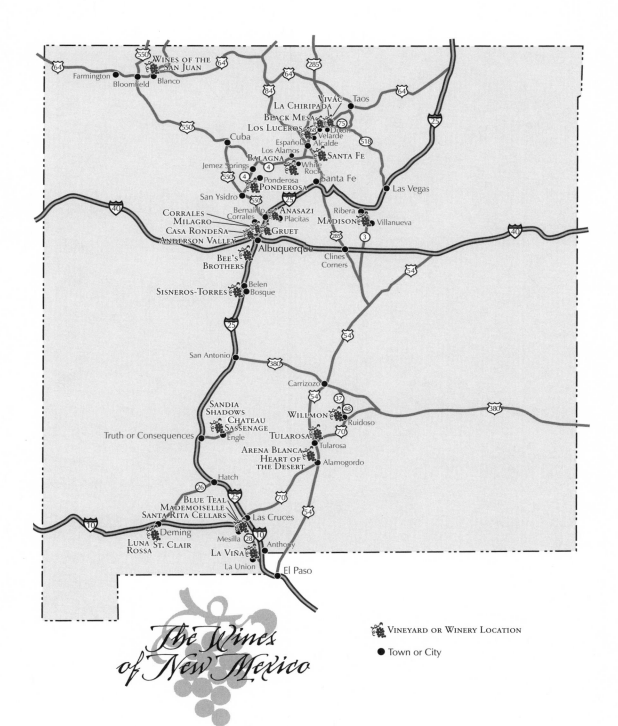

WINES OF THE
SAN JUAN

64 Farmington
    Bloomfield Blanco

550

64

285

84 VIVÁC Taos
    LA CHIRIPADA
    BLACK MESA
    LOS LUCEROS Dixon
                 Velarde
    Cuba   Española Alcalde
                 Los Alamos
    BALAGNA   SANTA FE
    Jemez Springs White
    550 4   Rock
         Ponderosa Santa Fe
    PONDEROSA
    San Ysidro   Las Vegas

40

    CORRALES   Bernalillo ANASAZI   Ribera
    MILAGRO   Corrales Placitas
    CASA RONDEÑA   MADISON Villanueva
    ANDERSON VALLEY GRUET
                     Albuquerque
    BEE'S   Clines
    BROTHERS   Corners

    SISNEROS-TORRES Belen
                     Bosque

40

54

    San Antonio
              380
         Carrizozo

    SANDIA   54   37
    SHADOWS   48
    CHATEAU   WILLMON Ruidoso
    SASSENAGE   70
    Truth or Consequences TULAROSA
              Engle   Tularosa
         ARENA BLANCA
         HEART OF
         THE DESERT Alamogordo

         Hatch

    26 25
    BLUE TEAL
    MADEMOISELLE 70
    SANTA RITA CELLARS Las Cruces 54
         Deming
    LUNA ST. CLAIR Mesilla 28 10 Anthony
    ROSSA   LA VIÑA
              La Union El Paso

*The Wines
of New Mexico*

🍇 VINEYARD OR WINERY LOCATION
● Town or City

5

ZONE 1

Southern Region

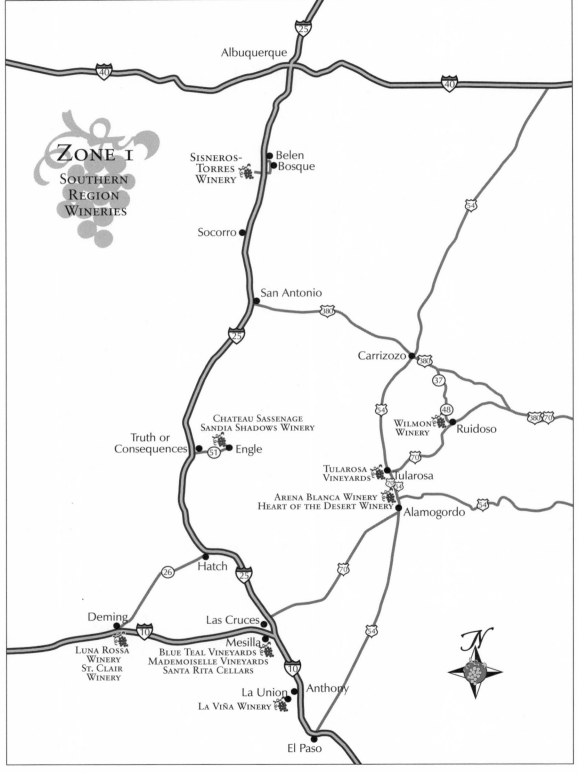

ZONE 1

SOUTHERN
REGION
WINERIES

Albuquerque

SISNEROS-
TORRES
WINERY
• Belen
• Bosque

Socorro

San Antonio

380

Carrizozo

CHATEAU SASSENAGE
SANDIA SHADOWS WINERY

Truth or
Consequences
51 • Engle

WILMON
WINERY
Ruidoso

TULAROSA
VINEYARDS
Tularosa

ARENA BLANCA WINERY
HEART OF THE DESERT WINERY
Alamogordo

26 Hatch
25

Deming
10
Las Cruces

Mesilla
BLUE TEAL VINEYARDS
MADEMOISELLE VINEYARDS
SANTA RITA CELLARS

LUNA ROSSA
WINERY
ST. CLAIR
WINERY

N

La Union
Anthony
LA VIÑA WINERY

El Paso

8

ZONE 1: SOUTHERN REGION ⁓

ZONE 1
SOUTHERN REGION WINERIES OF NEW MEXICO

Area south of I-40 along the Rio Grande to Deming, to the west of I-25, and to Alamogordo and Tularosa to the east

VICINITY OF:
paved roads to winery from nearest vicinity.

DISTANCES TO:
Miles to Vicinity

	Albuquerque	Farmington	Las Cruces	Clayton	Hobbs
Belen	34	216	189	307	322
(in Bosque southwest of Belen) Sisneros-Torres Winery					
Truth or Consequences	149	331	75	411	324
Chateau Sassenage Sandia Shadows Winery					
Mesilla	225	417	2	416	257
Mademoiselle Vineyards Tasting Room Santa Rita Cellars					
Las Cruces	223	415	—	414	255
Blue Teal Vineyards					
Anthony/La Union	251	443	28	442	283
La Viña Winery (in La Union)					
Deming	277	468	62	477	318
St. Clair Winery Luna Rossa Winery					
Ruidoso	191	373	114	330	187
Willmon Winery					
Alamogordo/Tularosa	208	411	69	351	17
Arena Blanca Tularosa Vineyards (in Tularosa, 13 miles north of Alamogordo) Heart of the Desert Winery					

9

Our Lady of Refuge Chapel, Belen, New Mexico.

10

Belen/Bosque

In the vicinity of Belen and Bosque, there is one winery and vineyard.
It is the Sisneros-Torres Winery.

Belen is a progressive town with a population of eleven thousand. It lies in the heart of the Middle Rio Grande Valley, thirty-four miles south of Albuquerque off I-25, at an elevation of 4,800 feet above sea level. It was founded in 1740 when two Spaniards, Diego Torres and Antonio Salazar, petitioned the governor of New Mexico in Santa Fe for a land grant. The request was granted and was known as *Nuestra Señora de Belén* (Our Lady of Belen). *Belén* is Spanish for "Bethlehem."

Twenty-four families settled on the land grant, farmed the fertile soil of the rich river bottomlands of the valley, and planted vineyards of grapes needed for their celebration of the Eucharist in the Catholic mass. When the railroad came, in the mid-1880s, it became the commercial center. Later, when the Santa Fe Railroad opened, the cut-off established Belen as its "hub city." Because of its central location in the state, Belen became a railroad center and an important shipping point for the agricultural products of the Rio Grande Valley. Dairying is now its growing industry, and acres of grape vineyards are flourishing throughout the area. Its location has an ideal climate for grape culture, with its hot days, cool nights, and a plentiful supply of water to produce the finest grapes in the area. Vacationers and health seekers are attracted by its ideal climate, and sportsmen, too, find it a convenient place to stop to hunt in the Manzano Mountains and to fish the irrigation ditches, which are stocked by the New Mexico Department of Game and Fish.

Today, Belen is a thriving city that has retained its country atmosphere. It has full accommodations and services for the visitor: restaurants, stores, hotels, a hospital, a library, schools, and a newspaper.

A few miles southwest of Belen is the small village of Bosque, which was founded during the eighteenth century as a settlement of *genízaros,* who were Christianized, captive Indians. They settled and farmed the area. Some of these small farms are still operating and owned by their descendants. They borrowed their irrigation systems from the early Pueblo Indians, who occupied the area before the conquistadors marched through the region. These *acequias* (irrigation ditches, connected by the main ditch) were dug and maintained by the community. About ten miles south of Bosque, off NM 116, is the ninety-acre vineyard and winery of the Sisneros-Torres family.

11

Sisneros-Torres Vineyards, Bosque, New Mexico.

SISNEROS-TORRES
VINEYARDS & WINERY

Ray Sisneros and his daughter, Bertha Sisneros-Torres, founded the Sisneros-Torres Winery in 1996. Ray Sisneros bought the first vineyard, and then increased the vineyard size from ten acres to one hundred acres. The vineyards and winery are located in the heart of the Rio Grande Valley where the fertile soil, plentiful water supply, hot days, and cool nights provide an ideal climate for production of the finest grapes in the area.

Because of the cold winters, a true vinifer cannot thrive in this location, so they buy some of their grapes from Deming, blending 20 percent of the true vinifer with their homegrown hybrids. Some of the hybrids produced in their own vineyards are Vidal Blanc, Chancellor, and Merlot.

They have sixty acres in production and forty acres in reserve. They crushed about twenty-four tons of grapes in 2003. Each ton produces 150 gallons, resulting in 2.5 gallons per case. Ray is the chief winemaker. His experience dates back to his first vines in 1948, when he planted twenty-five vines. He uses French oak barrels and stainless steel tanks in the production of some of the finest wines produced in the state. Their signature wine is a fine Cabernet Sauvignon. Another is their El Rojo, a super-dry and very popular red Merlot-type wine, very mild and very complementary with Mexican cuisine and pasta.

They presently produce six wines: El Rojo, Suprema, Vidal Blanc, Rosé, Vino Nativo, and Oro Blanco. They also produce a bubbly (sparkling wine).

See the facing page for more information on visiting hours and visitor facilities.

DIRECTIONS FROM ALBUQUERQUE:

Go south on I-25 and take exit 190.
Go 10 miles south on NM 116 and
follow the signs to the vineyards and winery.

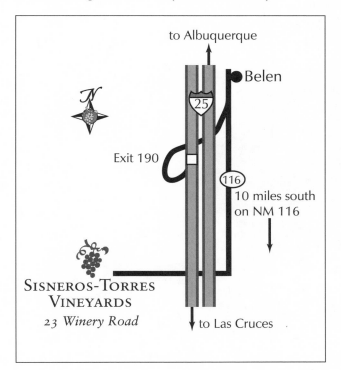

to Albuquerque

Belen

25

Exit 190

116

10 miles south
on NM 116

**SISNEROS-TORRES
VINEYARDS**

23 Winery Road

to Las Cruces

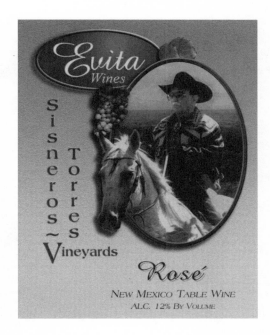

WINERY DETAILS:

Acres in Production: 60

Elevation: 6,500 feet

Hours: *by appointment*, 8 A.M.–6 P.M. (Sun. noon–6 P.M.)

Proprietor: Raymond F. and Eva Sisneros and Nash
    and Bertha Torres

Distance from Albuquerque: 45 miles
    (10 miles south of Belen)

Location: 23 Winery Road North, Bosque, NM 87006

Mailing Address: PO Box 193, Bosque, NM 87006

Telephone: (505) 861-3802

E-mail: bert9436@msn.com

Founded: 1996

Grape Varietals: Vidal Blanc, Chancellor, Merlot,
    Cabernet Sauvignon, El Rojo

Wine Types: dry red and white table wines,
    and dessert wine

Wine Procurement: Kelly Liquors, Quarters, Wild Oats,
    Walgreens, Wal-Mart

WINERY FACILITIES:

Tasting Room: Yes

Meeting Room: Yes

Picnic Site: No

Restrooms: Yes

Snacks: No

Lodgings: In Belen

*For information on Glassware and
Tasting, Wine Service and Cooking
with Wine, and Wine Storage, see
appendix Wine ABCs beginning
on page 110.*

13

Geronimo Springs Museum, Truth or Consequences, New Mexico.

14

Truth or Consequences

There are two wineries in the vicinity of Truth or Consequences.
They are Chateau Sassenage and Sandia Shadows. Both are located in
the small village of Engle, a short distance from Truth or Consequences.

Truth or Consequences is the county seat of Sierra County. The city was originally called Hot Springs, because of the hot mineral waters bubbling to the surface in the many springs in the area, which resulted from the tremendous upheavals of the earth millennia ago, draining the sea that once covered the Rio Grande Valley. Truth or Consequences is located 149 miles south of Albuquerque and is 4,269 feet above sea level. It is a friendly town of a little more than six thousand people, who enjoy its small-town atmosphere, moderate climate, and year-round recreational and social activities. Thousands flock to Truth or Consequences in any season to enjoy the pollution-free air, the sunny, dry climate, and the recreational opportunities offered at the two large lakes nearby: Elephant Butte and Caballo Lake. These advantages make Truth or Consequences an ideal retirement spot, where people can enjoy year-round golf, tennis, fishing, boating, good restaurants, and western-style nightlife. Visitors are also attracted to the many special events, such as the Easter weekend Hot Air Balloon Rally, the Hillsboro Apple Festival during Labor Day weekend, and the New Mexico State Old Time Fiddlers Contest in the fall.

The Truth or Consequences Fiesta in early May, featuring TV personality Ralph Edwards, has become a major annual event. Truth or Consequences became its legal name in 1950, when the top-rated nighttime radio show *Truth or Consequences*, hosted by Ralph Edwards, offered free publicity in the form of an annual fiesta to any town or city in the United States willing to change its name to Truth or Consequences. The small resort town of Hot Springs showed the most interest, and the residents voting for the name change won out over their opponents. From that point on, Ralph Edwards and his wife, Barbara, and other television and motion picture friends came each year to the promised Annual Fiesta Celebration. Ralph Edwards has also donated much of his memorabilia to the popular Geronimo Springs Museum on Main Street. The museum displays artifacts and arts and crafts indigenous to the area where visitors can become acquainted with history of the surrounding region. There are excellent accommodations and services for the visitor to Truth or Consequences.

15

Fermentation tanks at Chateau Sassenage. Photo courtesy Philippe Littot

CHATEAU SASSENAGE

*C*hateau Sassenage Vineyards and Winery was founded in 1983 by the Rostin family. They chose land along the Rio Grande Valley in the small village of Engle, east of Truth or Consequences and Elephant Butte Lake. The climate in this area is ideal for grape culture—hot days, cool nights, and plentiful water and sunshine. The vineyards and winery are now owned by Philippe Rostin, who employs Philippe Littot (Lee-toe) as chief winemaker and manager. Littot was born in Tunisia, a French colony in North Africa on the Mediterranean. He earned his oenology degree from Dijon University in Burgundy. Philippe Littot also owns and operates the Sandia Shadows Winery, featured on page 18, in the same location as Sassenage.

Today Chateau Sassenage is one of the largest grape-producing vineyards in New Mexico, covering an area of three hundred acres, and they supply many other wineries in the state. In order to obtain a high-quality product, they intentionally limit their production. They have fifty acres in production and use all of their own grapes in their wine production, with a high yield of Cabernet Sauvignon, Sauvignon Blanc, Chardonnay, a Blush, a Chablis, and a Merlot. They also produce a sparkling wine under the label of Monet-Jailon. In 1997 their Sauvignon was the Grand Champion of New Mexico wineries and they have won gold, silver, and bronze medals in various other competitions.

Depending on the weather they produce about ten thousand cases of wine annually. Chateau Sassenage uses both French oak and American oak barrels. Their wines are available for sale at all supermarkets and liquor stores in Albuquerque and in some outlets in Truth or Consequences.

The facing page lists more information.

16

DIRECTIONS FROM ALBUQUERQUE:

Go south on I-25 and take the T or C exit (Exit 79). Go east on NM 51 and continue 17 miles towards Engle. until you see a gate and sign for the Winery. Turn left through the gate onto a dirt road and continue until you come to the winery and vineyards. The winery is in a brown building.

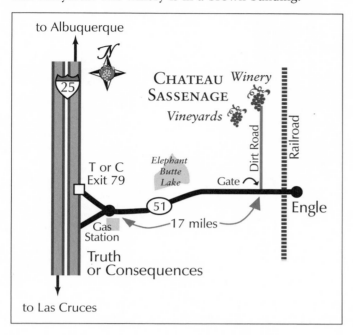

WINERY DETAILS:

Acres in Production: 50

Elevation: 5,000 feet

Hours: 9 A.M.–6 P.M. daily (*by appointment only*)

Proprietor: Philippe Rostin

Distance from Albuquerque: 158 miles

Location: Engle, New Mexico, approximately 18 miles south of Truth or Consequences and east of Elephant Butte Lake off I-25

Mailing Address: PO Box 1606, T or C, NM 87901

Telephone/Fax: (505) 856-1006

Founded: 1983 by the Rostin family

Grape Varietals: Cabernet Sauvignon, Chardonnay, Merlot

Wine Types: red and white table wines

Wine Procurement: all supermarkets and liquor stores in Albuquerque, some in T or C.

WINERY FACILITIES:

Tasting Room: Yes

Meeting Room: No

Picnic Site: No

Restrooms: Yes

Snacks: No

Lodgings: At T or C and Elephant Butte Lake

For information on Glassware and Tasting, Wine Service and Cooking with Wine, and Wine Storage, see appendix Wine ABCs beginning on page 110.

Sandia Shadows vintner, owner Phillipe Litott.

SANDIA SHADOWS
VINEYARD & WINERY

A brief discourse on wine education was my first introductory greeting by vintner Philippe Littot, owner and winemaker of Sandia Shadows Vineyard and Winery. With intense passion, his French accent punctuated with hand gestures lent colorful credibility to his subject. "Education," he said, "is a necessity in provoking interest in wine. We try to teach fundamentals. You must guide the people—you must address your book to the beginners. I suggest for the beginners not to start with dry wine. Try sweet wine first, because you can drink sweet wine anytime. Till you get used to drinking wine, then go to dry wine gradually—like beer, you can drink it anytime!" I could not have agreed more with this knowledgeable vintner's laconic simplification of just one area of a very complex subject, *tasting*. "With experience," he said, "we have blended the complex aromas and flavors of the popular Cabernet Sauvignon grape. The resulting texture and softness is the resulting end product of aging in selected oak barrels. The wine will complement both beef and pasta dishes and is an ideal accompaniment for New Mexican cuisine."

Philippe Littot was born in Tunisia, a French colony in North Africa on the Mediterranean. When he was three years old, his family moved to Corsica, a French Island north of Sardinia in the Mediterranean, where he lived until moving to Burgundy to earn a degree in oenology from Dijon University. He then came to the United States in 1983. He went to work as manager of grape production for one of the oldest and largest wineries in New Mexico, the Chateau Sassenage Winery, located in Engle, a small village east of Truth or Consequences. Philippe is still affiliated with Chateau Sassenage and recently moved his facility there and also serves as their chief winemaker. He produces a very good-quality Cabernet and a dry red table wine, along with a green chile wine—this wine has a spicy flavor and is very complementary with Mexican food. Chardonnay and Cabernet are his signature wines.

DIRECTIONS FROM ALBUQUERQUE:

Same as Chateau Sassenage, not currently open to the public.
Go south on I-25 and take the T or C exit (Exit 79). Go east
on NM 51 and continue 17 miles towards Engle. until you see
a gate and sign for the Winery. Turn left through the gate onto
a dirt road and continue until you come to the winery and
vineyards. The winery is in a brown building.

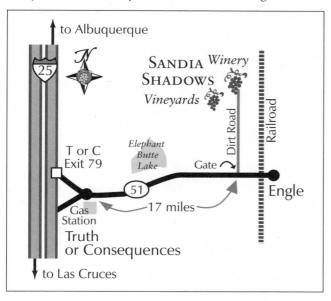

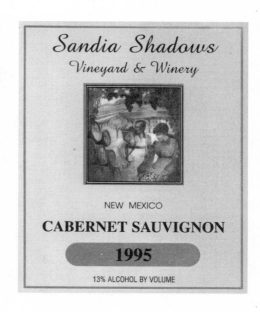

WINERY DETAILS:

Acres in Production: 50

Elevation: 5,000 feet

Hours: *by appointment only*

Proprietor: Philippe Littot

Distance from Albuquerque: 159 miles

Location: In Engle, about 20 miles east of T or C

Mailing Address: PO Box 92675, Albuquerque, NM 87199-2675

Telephone: (505) 856-1006

Fax: (505) 858-0859

E-mail: info@sandiawines.com

Founded: 1984 in Albuquerque

Grape Varietals: Chardonnay, Sauvignon Blanc, Cabernet
Sauvignon, Zinfandel

Wine Types: Sweet wines, red and white table wines.
Sandia Blush, Autumn Gold, Green Chile Wine,
Raspberry Wine, Sparkling Wine

Wine Procurement: on-site and in most liquor stores; restaurants
such as Carmen's, Artichoke Cafe, Wyndham Hotel restaurant

WINERY FACILITIES:

Tasting Room: No

Meeting Room: No

Picnic Site: No

Restrooms: Yes

Snacks: No

Lodgings: In T or C and
Elephant Butte

*For information on Glassware and
Tasting, Wine Service and Cooking
with Wine, and Wine Storage, see
appendix Wine ABCs beginning
on page 110.*

Fountain Theatre, built in 1905, Mesilla, New Mexico.
The oldest continuously operating theatre in New Mexico.

20

Las Cruces / Mesilla

In the vicinity of Las Cruces and Mesilla there are three tasting rooms owned by New Mexico Wineries, Inc., which is located in Deming and owned and operated by the Lescombes family. They are Blue Teal Vineyards, located in Las Cruces, the heart of the Mesilla Valley; and the Wines of New Mexico Tasting Rooms, featuring the Santa Rita Cellars and Mademoiselle labels, both located in historic Old Mesilla off the plaza next to the old Fountain Theatre. The Fountain Theatre, built in 1905, is the oldest continuously operating theatre in the state.

A variety of vacation pleasures await the visitor, who can sightsee or stroll on old plazas or along streets where legendary Wild West heroes and outlaws walked—characters like Billy the Kid and Sheriff Pat Garrett. And for those whose passions lean toward picturesque villages and thick-walled adobe buildings that once protected settlers from Apache attacks, Las Cruces is the place to visit. Here, one can imagine life as it might have been years ago.

Las Cruces lies in the heart of the fertile Mesilla Valley and has retained the charm and Old West flavor, as evident in the village of La Mesilla, a state monument two miles south of town, where colorful *ristras* of red chile, symbols of southwestern hospitality, decorate homes and businesses. It was in Mesilla that Billy the Kid received the death penalty at the county courthouse. He escaped jail and later was tracked down and killed by Sheriff Pat Garrett. The Las Cruces Masonic Cemetery, in downtown Las Cruces, holds the remains of Pat Garrett, who was ambushed and killed in 1908 in the nearby Organ Mountains.

Las Cruces is a thriving and growing city of more than sixty thousand, lying at an elevation of 3,900 feet above sea level. It was established as a city in 1907 and is bordered by the jagged Organ Mountains on the east, and the Rio Grande on the west. For centuries the Las Cruces site has been a stopping place for traveling parties. In 1598, Don Juan de Oñate led colonists along *El Camino Real* (the Royal Road or King's Highway). The journey started in the city of Chihuahua, Mexico, passed through Las Cruces, and continued to Santa Fe. It was along this route, a few miles north of the present site of Las Cruces, that Apaches attacked and killed a party of travelers from Taos, New Mexico. Subsequent travelers who found their bodies erected crosses to mark their graves. Other travelers who followed referred to the site as *La Placita de Las Cruces* (The Place of the Crosses). The name was later shortened to Las Cruces.

Today, Las Cruces lies in an area surrounded by chile farms, cotton fields, groves of pecan trees, and acres of vineyards. It is only fifty miles south to the colorful shops and markets of Juarez, Mexico, and only an hour's drive north to the major recreation spots of Elephant Butte Lake, Caballo Lake, and Percha Dam state parks. There is a full array of accommodations, conveniences, facilities, stores, and service stations for the visitor to Las Cruces and Mesilla.

21

Blue Teal Vineyards Tasting Room, Las Cruces, New Mexico.

BLUE TEAL VINEYARDS
TASTING ROOM

The Blue Teal Vineyards Tasting Room is located in Las Cruces, New Mexico, at the gateway to historic Mesilla in the heart of the Mesilla Valley. Herve Lescombes founded the Blue Teal Vineyards in 1980. During that same year he sold his Domaine de Perignon Vineyard in Burgundy, France. For three generations the Lescombes family had been winemakers in the French colony of Algeria, North Africa, until the revolution of 1961, which resulted in loss of their property and possessions. They returned to France and fifteen years later Herve and his father and brother Jean Paul built and established the Domaine de Perignon, the largest vineyard in the Burgundy region of France.

After the sale of Domaine de Perignon in 1980, Herve planted his first vineyard in Truth or Consequences. The following year he and his family moved to Lordsburg, New Mexico, and founded the Blue Teal Vineyards. Two years later they built a two-hundred-thousand-gallon winery at the vineyard and in 1985 crushed their first harvest and bottled their first wine under the Blue Teal Vineyards label. The Lescombes' knowledge and craft of fine winemaking has been honed over six generations and this expertise has been passed from Herve to his sons, Emanuel and Florent Lescombes, who are carrying on the long family tradition of world-class vintners. In addition to a wide variety of red and white wines, Blue Teal has added the DH Lescombes label, which includes premium oak barrel–aged Chardonnay, Cabernet, and fine sparkling wine. According to Peggy King, manager of the Blue Teal and Wines of the Southwest Tasting Rooms, located a short distance away off the Old Mesilla Plaza, their signature wine is considered to be the DH Lescombes Cabernet and the Blue Teal White Merlot. The White Merlot is a very popular fruity wine that goes well with spicy foods indigenous to the area. Another popular wine and bestseller is the Port, which also bears the DH Lescombes label.

For more information concerning this leader in the New Mexico wine industry, see St. Clair Winery, page 34.

22

DIRECTIONS FROM ALBUQUERQUE:

Take I-25 south to Las Cruces. Then go west on I-10 and take exit 140 (Avienda de Mesilla). Continue south to the tasting room at 1720 Avenida de Mesilla.

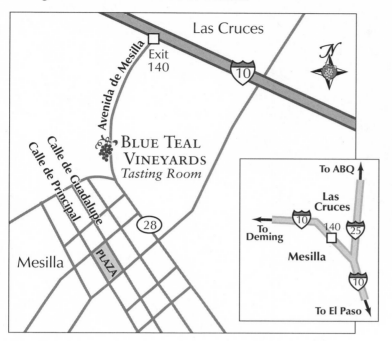

Blue Teal
VINEYARDS
2003
New Mexico
Muscat
PRODUCED & BOTTLED BY
NEW MEXICO WINERIES , INC., DEMING , NM
ALCOHOL 11.5% BY VOLUME

WINERY DETAILS:

Acres in Production: 72 in Deming

Elevation: 4,200 feet

Hours: Mon.–Sat. 11 A.M.–6 P.M., Sun. noon–6 P.M.

Proprietor: New Mexico Wineries, Inc. (the Lescombes family)

Distance from Albuquerque: 225 miles

Location: 1710 Avenida de Mesilla, Las Cruces, NM 88005; at the gateway to "Old Mesilla," Las Cruces, NM

Mailing Address: PO Box 1180, Deming, NM 88031

Telephone: (505) 524-0390 or (877) 669-4637

Fax: (505) 524-3579

E-mail: sales@BlueTeal.com

Website: www.BlueTeal.com

Founded: 1987 by Herve Lescombes

Grape Varietals: Chardonnay, Cabernet Sauvignon, White Merlot, Merlot, Zinfandel, Muscat, Sauvignon Blanc, Blanc de Blanc, White Zinfandel

Wine Types: table and sparkling wines

Wine Procurement: At tasting room. See Website for list of liquor and grocery stores

WINERY FACILITIES:

Tasting Room: Yes

Meeting Room: Yes

Picnic Site: Yes

Restrooms: Yes

Snacks: gift shop sells gourmet imported foods and cheeses

Lodgings: In town

For information on Glassware and Tasting, Wine Service and Cooking with Wine, and Wine Storage, see appendix Wine ABCs beginning on page 110.

23

Mademoiselle and Santa Rita Cellars (see page 26) Tasting Room, Mesilla, New Mexico.

MADEMOISELLE VINEYARDS
TASTING ROOM
(WINES OF THE SOUTHWEST)

The Mademoiselle Tasting Room is located next to the historic Fountain Theatre off the plaza in Old Mesilla. It shares the space with the Santa Rita Cellars label. Both labels are owned by New Mexico Wineries, Inc., located in Deming, New Mexico, under the proprietorship of the Lescombes family. The tasting room features all the labels of New Mexico Wineries, Inc. These wines are all made at the winery in Deming. Mademoiselle offers a selection of premium wines made only from New Mexico grapes grown on New Mexico Wineries' seventy-two-acre vineyards. The labels include Blue Teal Vineyards (see page 22), Mademoiselle, and Santa Rita Cellars (page 26). Also offered for sampling are the St. Clair and DH Lescombes labels.

Mademoiselle invites you to enjoy a free sample of these award-winning wines during your browsing through the art galleries and shops in beautiful and historic Old Mesilla at the edge of Las Cruces. (For more information on its founding and proprietorship, see St. Clair Winery on page 34.)

24

Directions from Albuquerque:

Take I-25 south to Las Cruces. Then go west on I-10 and take exit 140. Continue south on Avenida de Mesilla to the plaza. The tasting room is off the plaza, next to the Fountain Theatre, at 2641 Calle de Guadalupe. Mademoiselle Tasting Room shares space in this building with Santa Rita Cellars.

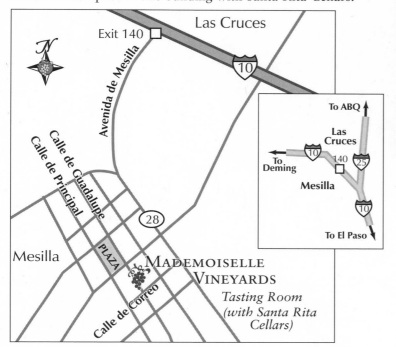

Winery Details:

Acres in Production: 72 acres in Deming

Elevation: 3,900 feet above sea level

Hours: Mon.–Sat. 11 A.M.–6 P.M., Sun. noon–6 P.M.; tours at 11:30 A.M. daily.

Proprietor: the Lescombes family

Distance from Albuquerque: 223 miles

Location: off the plaza in Old Mesilla

Mailing Address: 2641 Calle de Guadalupe, Mesilla, NM 88047

Telephone: (505) 524-2408 or (877) NM WINES

Website: www.mademoisellevineyards.com

Founded: 1981 by Herve Lescombes

Grape Varietals: Cabernet Sauvignon, Merlot, Muscat, Chardonnay, Zinfandel, Sauvignon Blanc, and Sparkling Wine

Wine Types: table, dessert, sparkling wine, and blends

Wine Procurement: at the winery and the tasting room

Winery Facilities:

Tasting Room: Yes

Meeting Room: No

Picnic Site: No

Restrooms: No

Snacks: No

Lodgings: In town

For information on Glassware and Tasting, Wine Service and Cooking with Wine, and Wine Storage, see appendix Wine ABCs beginning on page 110.

25

The Tasting Room for Mademoiselle and Santa Rita Cellars is next door to the historic Fountain Theater.

SANTA RITA CELLARS
(WINES OF THE SOUTHWEST)

The Santa Rita Cellars Tasting Room is located next to the historic Fountain Theatre, off the plaza in Old Mesilla. It shares space with the Mademoiselle Vineyards Tasting Room. Both labels are owned by New Mexico Wineries, Inc., located in Deming under the proprietorship of the Lescombes family. The tasting room features all the labels of New Mexico Wineries, Inc. These wines are all made at the winery in Deming. The tasting room offers a selection of premium wines made only from New Mexico grapes grown on New Mexico Wineries' seventy-two-acre vineyards. The labels include Blue Teal Vineyards, Mademoiselle Vineyards, and Santa Rita Cellars. Also offered for sampling are the other labels of New Mexico Wineries, Inc.: St. Clair and DH Lescombes. Santa Rita Cellars offers unique sparkling wines with exquisite champagne cocktail flavors that include Strawberry, Prickly Pear, and Sangria.

Santa Rita Cellars welcomes you to enjoy a free sample of these award-winning wines during your browsing through the art galleries and shops in beautiful, historic Old Mesilla on the edge of Las Cruces.

For more detailed information about its founding and proprietorship, see St. Clair Winery on page 34.

26

DIRECTIONS FROM ALBUQUERQUE:

Take I-25 south to Las Cruces. Then go west on I-10 and take exit 140. Continue south on Avenida de Mesilla to the plaza. The tasting room is off the plaza, next to the Fountain Theatre, at 2641 Calle de Guadalupe. Santa Rita Cellars shares space in this building with the Mademoiselle Tasting Room.

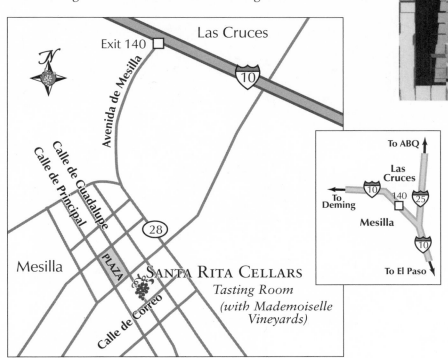

WINERY DETAILS:

Acres in Production: 72 in Deming

Elevation: 3,900 feet

Hours: Mon.–Sat. 11 A.M.–6 P.M., Sun. noon–6 P.M.

Proprietor: New Mexico Wineries, Inc. (Lescombes family)

Distance from Albuquerque: 223 miles

Location: off the plaza in Old Mesilla

Mailing Address: 2641 Calle de Guadalupe,
    Mesilla, NM 88047

Telephone: (505) 524-2408 or (877) NM WINES

Website: www.SantaRitaCellars.com

Founded: 1981 by Herve Lescombes

Grape Varietals: See Wine Types

Wine Types: bubbly beverages; champagne cocktail flavors
    include Strawberry, Sangria, and Prickly Pear

Wine Procurement: at winery and at tasting room

WINERY FACILITIES:

Tasting Room: Yes

Meeting Room: No

Picnic Site: No

Restrooms: No

Snacks: No

Lodgings: In town

For information on Glassware and Tasting, Wine Service and Cooking with Wine, and Wine Storage, see appendix Wine ABCs beginning on page 110.

27

La Viña Winery, La Union, New Mexico.

28

Anthony / La Union

Just south of Anthony and north of the border of Mexico is the small town of La Union and the home of La Viña Winery and Vineyards.

The town of Anthony lies astride the Texas–New Mexico border off I-10, where a sign boasts "The best town in 2 states." The town is in an area of thick-walled adobe buildings, Mission churches, cotton crops, and vineyards. Anthony is the gateway to New Mexico—it was founded in 1881. It began as a Santa Fe Railroad station. Its original name was La Tuna, Spanish for "prickly pear," which abounds in this area. The growth of the town extended on both sides of the border. Its name was later changed to Anthony as a dedication to the patron saint of an influential local Hispanic lady. About four miles north of Anthony along the scenic state highway NM 28, which parallels I-10 and passes through large spreads of irrigated pecan crops and vineyards, is the small village of La Union, where La Viña Winery—New Mexico's oldest winery—is located. Its vineyards date back to the planting of the vines by the missionaries and settlers who accompanied Don Juan de Oñate on his original route north.

Anthony has modern accommodations, food, and services for the tourist and the visitor, and side trips along the back roads offer a fascinating glimpse into the past.

29

The tasting roon at
La Viña Winery,
La Union, New Mexico.

LA VIÑA WINERY

La Viña Winery is located ten miles north of El Paso in the tiny village of La Union. It is situated in the fertile Mesilla Valley on the west side of the Rio Grande, where vines were planted by Franciscan missionaries who accompanied Don Juan de Oñate on his journey north through New Mexico in the late 1500s.

The original La Viña Winery was started in 1973 by Dr. Clarence Cooper, an associate professor of physics at the University of Texas at El Paso. He planted an experimental vine one mile south of the small village of Chamberino in 1973. After successful harvests of grapes that produced excellent wines, he increased production and opened the winery for business in 1977.

Denise and Ken Stark purchased the winery in 1992. The Starks operated a ranch and farm in the Texas Panhandle. After the sale of their operation, they settled in Albuquerque. Ken's interest in farming and winemaking led to an association with Anderson Valley Vineyards in Albuquerque, where he became assistant winemaker, then chief winemaker, and finally production manager. He also served as a consultant with other wineries, one of which was La Viña Winery. When La Viña went on the market in 1992, Ken and Denise's dream was fulfilled. They became owners of a 1,500-case operation and a vineyard producing sixty tons of grapes annually: Rieslings, Zinfandels, Cabernet Sauvignon, Chardonnay, and Sauvignon Blanc. In 1998 they relocated in the tiny village of La Union, five miles south of Chamberino, near Anthony, New Mexico. The vineyards in their present location were planted in 1998 and now consist of a total of forty acres, with twenty-five acres in production. All their wines are produced from their own cultivations. In 2003, they crushed more than seventy tons and produced about 4,500 cases.

As chief winemaker, Ken Stark has no assistants. With quality production in mind, his huge investment in French oak barrels for aging his dry wines, Chardonnays, and Sauvignon Blanc has resulted in many awards in wine-judging competitions. The main outlet for La Viña wine sales is at the winery tasting room. Wines can also be purchased at Kelly Liquors and Quarters in Albuquerque, and at some restaurants in Las Cruces. Their bestseller is La Dolce, a sparkling sweet Muscat. It is a wonderful dessert wine, very popular for parties. Another bestseller is their La Piñata, a delightful sparkling wine—a blend of Ruby Cabernet and White Zinfandel. Along with their other popular seller, Rojo Loco, many other varietals and blends are offered for tasting at the winery tasting room.

DIRECTIONS FROM ALBUQUERQUE:

Take I-25 south to Las Cruces. Take I-10 east (south) towards El Paso. Take the Vinton exit off I-10 and go east on Vinton Road/South Vinton Road to Highway 28. Go north on Highway 28, 1 mile to winery.

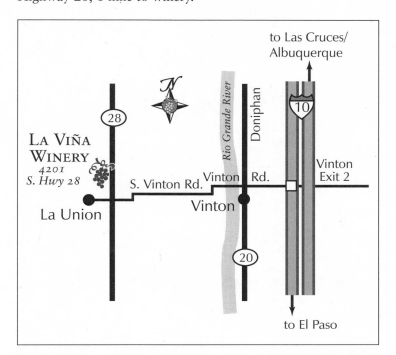

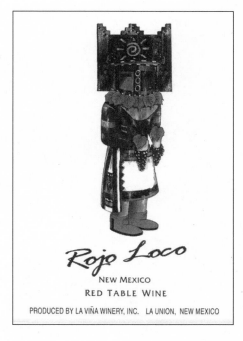

WINERY DETAILS:

Acres in Production: 25

Elevation: 4,000 feet

Hours: Mon.–Sat. 11 A.M.–5 P.M., Sun. noon–5 P.M.
Tours at 11:30 A.M. daily.

Proprietors: Denise and Ken Stark

Distance from Albuquerque: 250 miles

Location: 10 miles north of El Paso on Highway 28

Mailing Address: 4201 S. Highway 28, La Union, NM 88021

Telephone/Fax: (505) 882-7632

E-mail: lavinastar@aol.com

Founded: 1977 by Clarence Cooper; 1992 by
Denise and Ken Stark.

Grape Varietals: Chardonnay, Riesling, Zinfandel,
Cabernet Sauvignon, Merlot, Sauvignon Blanc, Muscat

Wine Types: table, sparkling, dessert

Wine Procurement: At Kelly Liquors and Quarters in
Albuquerque, in some restaurants in Las Cruces,
and at the tasting room in La Union

WINERY FACILITIES:

Tasting Room: Yes

Meeting Room: No

Picnic Site: Can accommodate
5,000. Hosts Harvest Festival
and Grape Stomp each year in
October and a Blues & Jazz
Festival in April, as well as an
old-fashioned country picnic
and open house on July 4.

Restrooms: Yes

Snacks: No

Lodgings: In El Paso

For information on Glassware and Tasting, Wine Service and Cooking with Wine, and Wine Storage, see appendix Wine ABCs beginning on page 110.

31

The tasting room at St. Clair Winery, Deming, New Mexico.

32

Deming

There are two wineries in the vicinity of Deming: Luna Rossa Winery and St. Clair Winery.

"The Home of Pure Water and Fast Ducks," read some of the billboard ads that greet visitors as they arrive in Deming. It is a town with a population of approximately fourteen thousand, located sixty miles west of Las Cruces off I-10, and is the Luna County Seat. Deming is a mecca for retirees who find its climate a pleasant escape from the harsh northern and eastern winters. It sits at an elevation of 4,335 feet above sea level. Its summer nighttime temperature averages in the mid to high sixties and day temperatures in the mid to high nineties. Winter temperatures sometimes drop below freezing at night, but rise to the mid to high fifties during the day. Deming boasts an annual 350 to 360 days of sunshine and an annual precipitation of 8.5 inches.

When the Southern Pacific Railroad built its shops and station, the site was called New Chicago. Later, during its founding in October 1881, it was renamed in honor of Mary Ann Deming, the daughter of an influential promoter of the Southern Pacific Railroad. Tents and shacks, stores and gambling houses spread rapidly around the station and with the arrival of the Santa Fe Railroad and completion of its junction with the Southern Pacific, the tents and shacks were replaced with more modern structures. The town flourished and became an important rail center. Its plentiful supply of water established Deming as a major cattle range with huge stretches of grassland and farms of cotton crops. The water's source came from the Rio Mimbres, twenty miles north of the town where it mysteriously vanished beneath the surface and continued its flow underground, finally emerging and draining into a lake in the southern Chihuahua desert.

With its main businesses of saloons and gambling houses came lawlessness. The outlaws and gunfighters, resentful Apaches who raided the settlers' homes and ranches, and warring factions of the competing railroads created a dangerous and hostile environment in a once peaceful oasis in the desert. Peaceful times finally replaced the turmoil as churches and civilization replaced the saloons and gambling bistros.

Though manganese is still mined, the mining of gold, silver, and copper no longer exists in the surrounding mountains of the Floridas to the southwest, Cook's Peak to the north, and Tres Hermanas (Three Sisters) to the south. No longer invaded by prospectors for gold, these rugged mountains, some rising more than eight thousand feet, create an enchanting frame for this bustling town in the heart of the desert.

There are many attractions in Deming. The most famous is the Great American Duck Race with a purse of $7,500. This event is gaining more popularity each year. Also popular is the coronation of the Duck Queen. The thirsty tourist may also visit the popular wineries in the area. The award-winning wineries of St. Clair, Blue Teal, and the newest, Luna Rossa, are detailed on the following pages.

Modern accommodations and services, food and gas stations, plus other attractions are available for the traveler.

33

*St. Clair Winery,
Deming, New Mexico.*

ST. CLAIR WINERY

St. Clair Winery is located four miles east of Deming on Old Highway 549. It is New Mexico's largest winery and the sixty-ninth largest winery in the United States. It had its beginnings in 1982 when a group of European vintners and investors came to New Mexico, where the land was less expensive than the high cost of available acreage in Europe. They found the Rio Grande and Mesilla valleys ideal for grape culture, so with their winemaking skills and the ideal climate of hot, sunny days and cool nights, they planted large expanses of vineyards. In those early years, St. Clair was the largest winery and vineyard operation in the Southwest and New Mexico. They built a huge facility with rows of European-style steel tanks for fermentation and a stemmer-crusher capable of crushing two hundred tons per day.

The present facility in the Mimbres Valley uses about 60 percent of its own grapes and continues to plant fifteen acres of grapes per year. They grow about sixteen different varieties, including Chardonnay and Cabernets. Their other labels and tasting rooms include Blue Teal, Mademoiselle, and Santa Rita—all located in the Las Cruces and Mesilla area of southern New Mexico. In 2002, St. Clair crushed 650 tons, yielding thirty-five hundred cases.

Florent Lescombes is a sixth-generation member of a winemaking family who came to the United States in late 1970 from the Chablis and Burgundy districts of France. Florent, a tall, affable young man, is the chief winemaker with three assistants. Florent came to this country when he was eleven years old. He uses French oak barrels for the Chardonnays, Cabernets, and Sauvignon Blanc. The wines are sold in all Albuquerque supermarkets and retail liquor stores under the St. Clair, Blue Teal, and Lescombes labels. They are all made at the St. Clair Winery in Deming. They service all their outlets directly, monitoring the shelves to insure the freshness of the wine to be sold. Their signature wine is sold under the Lescombes label.

For more details on the St. Clair Winery's visiting hours and facilities, see the facing page.

DIRECTIONS FROM ALBUQUERQUE:

Take I-25 south to Las Cruces, then go west on I-10 to Deming. Before reaching Deming take exit 85 off I-10 (just past the Holiday Inn). Go south to the junction of NM 549, then left, and continue 3 miles to the winery at 1325 De Baca Road SE.

Note: There is a short-cut to Deming from Albuquerque. Take I-25 south to the Hatch exit (Exit 41), where a sign directs traffic to Deming. Take NM 26 to Deming. When you reach Deming, go east on I-10 to exit 85 and follow above directions to the winery.

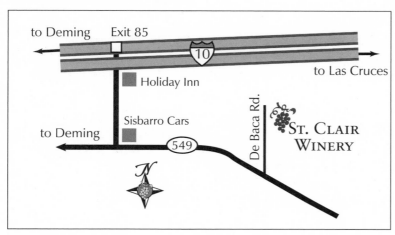

WINERY DETAILS:

Acres in Production: 74

Elevation: 4,400 feet

Hours: Mon.–Sat. 9 A.M.–6 P.M., Sun. noon–5 P.M.
 Free tours on Sat. at 11 A.M. & 3 P.M.

Proprietor: Herve Lescombes and family

Distance from Albuquerque: 277 miles

Location: 4 miles east of Deming

Mailing Address: 1325 De Baca Rd. SE, Deming, NM 88030

Telephone: (505) 546-9324 or (866) 336-7357

E-mail: sales@stclairvineyards.com

Website: www.stclairvineyards.com

Founded: by Herve Lescombes in the late 1970s

Grape Varietals: 16 varieties, including Chardonnays, Cabernets, Zinfandels, Rieslings, Sauvignons, Merlots, and Muscats

Wine Types: table and blends

Wine Procurement: All Albertsons supermarkets and retail liquor stores. Sold under St. Clair and Blue Teal labels

WINERY FACILITIES:

Tasting Room: Yes

Meeting Room: Yes

Picnic Site: Yes

Restrooms: Yes

Snacks: cheeses and jellies are sold

Lodgings: In town

For information on Glassware and Tasting, Wine Service and Cooking with Wine, and Wine Storage, see appendix Wine ABCs beginning on page 110.

35

Luna Rossa Winery

Luna Rossa is one of the newest wineries in New Mexico, but its experience in producing quality wine dates back to 1987. It is owned and operated by Sylvia and Paolo D'Andrea and located just west of Deming in the middle of the Mimbres Valley. All the grapes used in their wines come from New Mexico Vineyards Inc., the largest vineyard in New Mexico, which consists of three hundred acres, producing thirty-five varieties of grapes. This vineyard supplies seventeen different New Mexico wineries plus four wineries in Texas.

Luna Rossa is in its final stages of construction, but they have already produced about seven thousand gallons of wine under the Luna Rossa license. The chief winemaker is a wine consultant who is assisted by owner and manager Paolo D'Andrea. They use French and American oak barrels for the Chardonnay, Cabernet Sauvignon, Zinfandels, and Merlots. Even in its early stage of operation, Luna Rossa promises to become one of the outstanding wineries in New Mexico, offering wines made from Italian, German, Rhone, and Spanish varieties, all grown by New Mexico Vineyards Inc.

Visitors are welcome to the winery's tasting room. There is a picnic site and a meeting room in Luna Rossa's future plans. For more information on its facilities, see the facing page.

36

DIRECTIONS FROM ALBUQUERQUE:

From Albuquerque go south on I-25 to Las Cruces. Then go west on I-10 to Deming. Take exit 81 off I-10 then turn right (south) onto 13th street. Turn right (west) onto Frontage Road. Turn left (south) onto Skyview Road. Follow signs to winery.

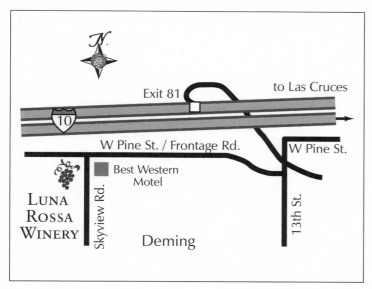

2002

New Mexico

Malvasia Bianca

Alc. 11.5% by Vol.   Mimbres Valley

WINERY DETAILS:

Acres in Production: 300

Elevation: 4,400 feet

Hours: Mon.–Sat. 10 A.M.–5 P.M., Sun. 1–5 P.M.

Proprietor: Sylvia and Paolo D'Andrea

Mailing Address: PO Box 1507, Deming, NM 88031

Distance from Albuquerque: 230 miles

Location: Deming, NM

Telephone: (505) 546-9324

E-mail: dandrea@zianet.com

Website: www.lunarossawinery.com

Founded: 2003

Grape Varietals: 26, including Chardonnays, Cabernets, Merlot, Zinfandels, Rieslings, and many others

Wine Types: table and blends

Wine Procurement: at winery

WINERY FACILITIES:

Tasting Room: Yes

Meeting Room: Yes

Picnic Site: Yes

Restrooms: Yes

Snacks: Yes

Lodgings: 1 mile away in Deming

For information on Glassware and Tasting, Wine Service and Cooking with Wine, and Wine Storage, see appendix Wine ABCs beginning on page 110.

37

View of Sierra Blanca, Ruidoso, New Mexico.

38

Ruidoso

There are two wineries/tasting rooms in Ruidoso, the Willmon Vineyards End of the Vine and the Viva New Mexico Tasting Rooms.

Ruidoso is located in the southeast corner of Lincoln County at the foot of Old Baldy Peak, forty-one miles southeast of Carrizozo. It is a year-round resort town 6,911 feet above sea level, with a population of about nine thousand, and is billed as "the playground of the Southwest." Ruidoso is also home of the All American Futurity Quarter Horse Race, offering a $1,035,900 purse, held annually on Labor Day. *Ruidoso* means "noisy," taking its name from the swift-running stream that runs through the town. It was here in the 1880s that the stream powered a gristmill known as Dowlin's Mill. Dowlin's Mill was the original name of the town.

If getting close to nature is your whim, then Ruidoso is the place to visit and enjoy anytime of the year. Each year, thousands of visitors are attracted to the Ruidoso area, where recreational opportunities abound. You can ski, fish, bike, or camp in the several sites scattered through this scenic mountain town. There are snow-clad mountains in the winter and changing colors of aspens that swath the surrounding forests in red, yellow, and gold in the fall. Sixteen miles from Ruidoso, by way of a good paved road, is the Sierra Blanca Ski Area. It is on the Mescalero Apache Indian Reservation and is equipped with full facilities, including a restaurant and tavern, a warming lodge, and an equipment rental shop. The town of Ruidoso has full facilities and accommodations for overnighters. There are more than seventy hotels and lodges, including supper clubs, restaurants, swimming pools, tennis courts, golf courses, riding stables, playgrounds, antique shops, gift shops, and it is the home of the Willmon Vineyards End of the Vine and Viva New Mexico Tasting Rooms.

The many camping, hunting, and cold and clear fishing streams and lakes are within a five- to ten-minute drive from town, making Ruidoso a sportsman's paradise. Just three miles south of Ruidoso, in a spectacular forested setting at an elevation of 7,200 feet, is the luxurious resort hotel, Inn of the Mountain Gods, located on the Mescalero Apache Indian Reservation and owned and operated by the tribe. This beautifully designed and appointed complex offers the ultimate in modern and attractive facilities, a restaurant, gift shops, and many recreational packages for guests.

39

*Willmon Vineyards
tasting room,
"End of the Vine,"
Ruidoso, New Mexico.*

WILLMON VINEYARDS

The Willmon Vineyards tasting rooms are located in the heart of beautiful downtown Ruidoso. Both are located within walking distance of each other. The Viva New Mexico Tasting Room offers sampling of not only the wines produced by Willmon, but also those produced by other wineries in New Mexico. The other tasting room is called End of the Vine. It is one of the finest and most attractive tasting rooms and gift shops in the state. End of the Vine offers everything to please the taste—gourmet imported cheese, fine stemware, and unique gift items. Visitors can sample wines at the attractive wine bar or relax at one of the tables as they enjoy the free samples of the wines that are offered.

Scott Willmon founded Willmon Vineyards in 1996 in the Deming area. His first vintage was produced in 1998. Scott's passion for wine and winemaking goes back to his early years of working for the Lescombes family's vineyards and winery. Scott always believed that New Mexico could produce a great wine and he has dedicated his efforts in winemaking toward that goal. With a little more than twenty acres in production, he grows about 80 percent of the grapes used in his wine. He grows about twenty varietals, but buys some from New Mexico Wineries, Inc., and from other New Mexico growers. In 2003 they crushed about fifty-five tons, producing about four thousand cases. Scott is the chief winemaker. He uses oak barrels to age his premium wines. Willmon Vineyards' signature wines are their Chardonnay and Quatro Reserve, a very fine Cabernet vintage. It is a wonderful refined blend of Cabernet Sauvignon, Cabernet Franc, Merlot, and Syrah. Their 2001 vintage is a full, fruity, great wine—smooth, with a full bouquet. It sets a standard for elegant red wine. Willmon's best-selling red wine is their Ruidoso Red. Their best-selling *wine* is their Chardonnay. (The number of cases sold annually is 2,500.)

40

Willmon's first international award was from the *Dallas Morning News* Wine Competition for their late-harvest Riesling. They have also won gold and silver at New Mexico State Fair competitions. The Willmon wines can be purchased at their tasting rooms, at liquor stores in Albuquerque and Santa Fe and throughout New Mexico, and at many restaurants. See the facing page for more information on tasting room facilities and hours.

DIRECTIONS FROM ALBUQUERQUE:

Take I-25 south to San Antonio and take Exit 139. Go east onUS 380. Continue past Carrizozo to NM 37 and turn south (right). Continue on NM 37 and until it merges with NM 48, and continue south on NM 48 to Ruidoso. Follow NM 48 / Mechem Dr. through the city of Ruidoso, until NM 48 becomes Sudderth Dr. The End of the Vine is in a shopping center on Sudderth Dr.

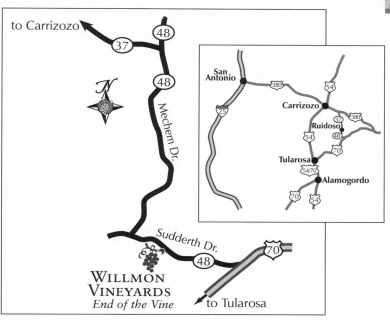

WINERY DETAILS:

Acres in Production: 20 in Deming
Elevation: 6,950 feet (Ruidoso tasting rooms)
Hours: Mon.–Sat. 10 A.M.–7 P.M., Sun. noon–6 P.M.
Proprietor: Wines of New Mexico, Inc.
Distance from Albuquerque: 189 miles
Location: Ruidoso
Mailing Address: 2801 Sudderth Dr., Ruidoso, NM 88345
Telephone: (505) 630-WINE
E-mail: jessica@winesofnewmexico.com
Website: www.winesofnewmexico.com
Founded: winery founded in 1996
Grape Varietals: more than twenty of the major varietals, including Cabernets, Sauvignons, Merlots, Chardonnays, etc.
Wine Types: sparkling, table, and dessert wines
Wine Procurement: in liquor stores throughout New Mexico (mostly in Albuquerque), at the tasting rooms, and in many restaurants

WINERY FACILITIES:

Tasting Room: two tasting rooms, both in Ruidoso
Meeting Room: in tasting room (End of the Vine), accommodates thirty
Picnic Site: No
Restrooms: Yes
Snacks: cheeses and snacks available
Lodgings: within walking distance of tasting rooms

For information on Glassware and Tasting, Wine Service and Cooking with Wine, and Wine Storage, see appendix Wine ABCs beginning on page 110.

41

St. Francis de Paula Church, Tularosa, New Mexico.

42

Alamogordo / Tularosa

In the vicinity of Alamogordo there are two wineries. They are Arena Blanca Winery and Heart of the Desert Winery. In the vicinity of Tularosa there is one: the Tularosa Vineyards and Winery.

Alamogordo is the seat of Otero County and is the largest town in the Tularosa Basin, with a population of more than twenty-nine thousand. It is located at the northern end of the Tularosa Basin astride Highway 54/70 with the looming Sacramento Mountains to the east and the White Sands desert expanse to the west. Alamogordo has a rich history steeped in western folklore, fierce Apache Indian raids on the settlers, and lawlessness. Spanish conquistadors and their accompanying missionaries settled along the lush, fertile Rio Grande Valley, and some planted Mission grapes and crops along the river. The cool nights and warm days in this area provide an ideal climate for planting vineyards of the grapes they needed for the wine used to celebrate the Eucharist. In the early 1880s, a Frenchman, Francois-Jean Rochas (called Frenchy), was the first to settle in Dog Canyon, located two miles east of present-day highway US 54 just south of Alamogordo. It is a lush, fertile, green oasis along a clear running stream. Frenchy built a crude cabin here, planted a fruit orchard and a vineyard, and raised cattle. He had control of the water, which led to disputes with neighboring ranchers over water rights. In 1894 he was found dead from gunshot wounds. The coroner's jury judged the apparent murder to be a suicide. Frenchy's cabin is still there serving as a tourist attraction.

Alamogordo had its beginnings in 1893 when Charles Eddy's dream of establishing a railroad through the Tularosa Basin to El Paso, Texas, was realized in 1897, when a group of investors decided to back his proposal. In 1898 he incorporated the El Paso and Northeastern Railroad. The town flourished, becoming a large ranching and farming center. It vaulted into the twentieth century when on July 16, 1945, at Trinity Site, northeast of the city, the first atom bomb exploded. The huge expanse of desert was an ideal site for a bombing range, which led to the building of the Alamogordo Air Force Base to train B-17 and B-24 bomber crews. Later, after the war, it became Holloman Air Force Base, serving as the U.S. Air Force Research and Development Command.

Just thirteen miles north of Alamogordo is the town of Tularosa, settled in the mid-1800s, where a network of ditches (acequias) were dug to irrigate the crops and vineyards planted by the early settlers and missionaries.

Both Alamogordo and Tularosa have modern facilities and accommodations to serve tourists and visitors to the area.

43

*Tularosa Winery and
Tasting Room,
Tularosa, New Mexico.*

TULAROSA
VINEYARDS & WINERY

The Tularosa Vineyards and Winery is located 2.5 miles north of Tularosa, just off New Mexico Highway 54. It is a family-owned business operated by the Wickham family. Dave Wickham was born on a farm near Watkins Glen in the Finger Lakes region of New York. His fondness for grape growing stems from his childhood memories of his family's winery. When Dave retired from the Air Force in the 1980s, he settled in Tularosa and planted some vines as a hobby. His initial plantings produced some very fine grapes, so in 1985 he purchased ten acres north of Tularosa, planted vine cuttings, converted an old abandoned military building into a winery, and in 1989 bottled his first wine.

Dave's Cabernets and Merlots became popular very quickly, winning awards in 1990, 1991, and 1992 at the Southwest Wine Competition. Today the Wickhams grow some of their own grapes on seven acres and buy some, mostly from local growers. All their grapes are New Mexico–grown. In 2002, they crushed about eighty tons and produced about two thousand cases. Dave's son Christopher is the chief winemaker. Christopher started at the winery while a student at college and earned a degree in international business. Like his father, he decided to become a winemaker and under Dave's guidance started learning the trade from the ground up. John Bennet, a chemist, is their tasting expert. They process about thirteen varieties of grapes. Their Chardonnays and all their red wines, such as their Merlot and Cabernet Sauvignon, are finished in oak barrels. They are primarily varietals produced from vinifer grapes and include most of the standard as well as some very informal varieties.

Picnic tables are available under the shade of beautiful pecan trees adjacent to the winery. Visitors are welcome for tours, tasting, and sales—all available at the winery daily, year-round. Tours are available by appointment.

See the facing page for quick reference to their facilities and accommodations.

44

Directions from Albuquerque:

Take I-25 south to San Antonio and take Exit 139. Go east on US 380. Continue 66 miles to Carrizozo, then south on US 54 to Tularosa. Go east on Coyote Canyon Road and follow signs to winery.

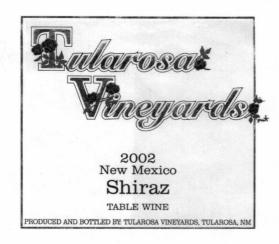

2002
New Mexico
Shiraz
TABLE WINE

PRODUCED AND BOTTLED BY: TULAROSA VINEYARDS, TULAROSA, NM

Winery Details:

Acres in Production: 7

Elevation: 4,600 feet

Hours: Noon–5 P.M. daily, tours by appointment

Proprietor: David Wickham

Distance from Albuquerque: 203 miles

Location: Two miles north of Tularosa, off US 54

Mailing Address: 23 Coyote Canyon Rd., Tularosa, NM 88352

Telephone: (505) 585-2260 or (800) 687-4467

E-mail: wine@nmex.com

Website: www.tularosavineyards.com

Founded: Winery 1989, first plantings 1985

Grape Varietals: Chardonnay, Cabernets, Merlot, Grenache, Mission, Zinfandel, Sauvignon Blanc, Chenin Blanc, and others

Wine Types: table, white, red, and blends

Wine Procurement: Wal-Mart, Kelly Liquors, Quarters, Cost Plus, Albertsons in Albuquerque, and Albertsons and Kelly Liquors in Santa Fe

Winery Facilities:

Tasting Room: holds 20 people

Meeting Room: tasting room serves as meeting room

Picnic Site: three tables under shade trees

Restrooms: Yes

Snacks: No

Lodgings: bed and breakfast and motel

For information on Glassware and Tasting, Wine Service and Cooking with Wine, and Wine Storage, see appendix Wine ABCs beginning on page 110.

45

Arena Blanca Winery and Tasting Room, Alamogordo, New Mexico.

ARENA BLANCA WINERY

*T*he Arena Blanca Winery and vineyards are located in the Tularosa Basin, surrounded by mountains, white sands, and the McGinn family's beautiful pistachio orchard. Tom McGinn and his son, Tim, originally founded the pistachio farm in 1978. It then became a federally licensed winery in 1999. In 1997, Tom and Tim planted Merlot, Chardonnay, Cabernet Sauvignon, and Gewurztraminer vines in the nine-acre vineyard. The first harvest in August of 1999 produced one thousand pounds of Chardonnay and Cabernet. It was followed three years later by another harvest of Merlot and Gewurztraminer varietals. They now have fourteen acres of grapes in production. Their production is steadily increasing and they expect to harvest four more acres in 2005.

Both Tom and Tim are the winemakers. Tom has a degree in technology from the University of California at Davis, and has thirty years of experience as an amateur winemaker. Tim has also taken educational courses at the University of California at Davis, in the fields of oenology and viniculture. They have no assistants. They use oak barrels for the Chardonnay and Cabernets for primary fermentation. Their wines can be purchased from two retailers, which are located around Alamogordo in the pistachio–farm store/gift shops, which they own. These gift shops also contain tasting rooms.

The McGinns consider two of their wines their signature wines. Both are consistent award winners in wine competitions. They are Cabernet Sauvignon and Pistachio Delight, a unique blend with pistachio flavor added to it. See the facing page for details on the winery's facilities, hours, and accommodations.

46

DIRECTIONS FROM ALBUQUERQUE:

Take I-25 south to San Antonio and take Exit 139.
Go east on US 380. Continue 66 miles to Carrizozo, then
south on US 54 through Tularosa towards Alamogordo.
The winery is at 7320 US 54/70 North.

WINERY DETAILS:

Acres in Production: 14

Elevation: 4,500 feet

Hours: Mon.–Sat. 9 A.M.–5 P.M., Sun. 10 A.M.–6 P.M.
(wine tasting/sales begin at noon on Sunday)

Proprietor: Tom and Tim McGinn

Mailing Address: 7320 US Hwy 54/70 North,
Alamogordo, NM 88301

Distance from Albuquerque: 216 miles

Location: 9 miles north of Alamogordo,
7 miles south of Tularosa

Telephone: (505) 437-0602

E-mail: info@pistachiotreeranch.com

Website: www.pistachiotreeranch.com

Founded: In 1999 by father and son, Tom and Tim McGinn

Grape Varietals: Cabernet Sauvignon, Chardonnay, Zinfandel,
Gewurztraminer, Merlot

Wine Types: table and dessert wines

Wine Procurement: at their two farm stores; in and
around Alamogordo

WINERY FACILITIES:

Tasting Room: Yes

Meeting Room: No

Picnic Site: grass, trees, and tables

Restrooms: handicapped, male
and female

Snacks: pistachio, vanilla, and
strawberry ice cream;
pistachio candy

Lodgings: in Alamogordo,
6 miles south of winery

*For information on Glassware and
Tasting, Wine Service and Cooking
with Wine, and Wine Storage, see
appendix Wine ABCs beginning
on page 110.*

47

Heart of the Desert
Tasting Room, in
Eagle Ranch gift shop,
Alamogordo,
New Mexico.

HEART OF THE DESERT
VINEYARD & TASTING ROOM

The Heart of the Desert Tasting Room is located just north of Alamogordo off US highway 54/70 in the gift shop of Eagle Ranch Pistachio Groves, a family-owned farm and New Mexico's first and largest producer of pistachios. This successful agribusiness is owned and operated by George and Marianne Schweers, is totally self-contained, and is blessed with an ideal climate for grape culture. It was natural, then, to add a vineyard to its operation.

They planted their vines in 2003. The plantings included Cabernet Sauvignon, Shiraz, Zinfandel, Chardonnay, and Merlot. Eighty acres are presently in production and they have high expectations of harvesting a fine yield in 2006. Until then, their wine is being produced by their chief winemaker, Scott Willmon, who has been in the winemaking business for eight years and whose own vineyards are located in Deming. (The Willmon tasting rooms are featured on page 40.)

The wines are fermented in stainless steel tanks, and the Muscat and Cabernet Sauvignon are recipients of numerous awards. Another award winner is their popular signature wine, the Pistachio Blush, which is a pistachio-flavored blend. Other favorites are listed on the facing page. Their wines can be purchased at the Eagle Ranch Pistachio Farms in Alamogordo and at Kelly Liquors in Albuquerque.

For more information on the Heart of the Desert Vineyard and Tasting Room, see the facing page.

48

DIRECTIONS FROM ALBUQUERQUE:

Take I-25 south to San Antonio and take Exit 139. Go east on US 380. Continue 66 miles to Carrizozo, then south on US 54 through Tularosa towards Alamogordo, and follow the signs to the Eagle Ranch Pistachio Farms and tasting room at 7288 US 54/70.

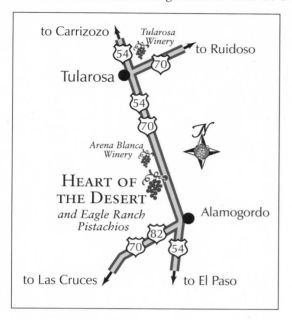

WINERY DETAILS:

Acres in Production: 50

Elevation: 4,000 feet

Hours: Sunday 9 A.M.–6 P.M.

Proprietor: George and Marianne Schweers

Distance from Albuquerque: 216 miles

Location: about 8 miles north of Alamogordo

Mailing Address: 7288 US Hwy 54/70, Alamogordo, NM 88310

Telephone: (505) 434-0035 or (800) 432-0999

E-mail: sales@eagleranchpistachios.com

Website: www.eagleranchpistachios.com

Founded: In 2003; the wines are made by Willmon Vineyards (See page 40.)

Grape Varietals: Cabernet Sauvignon, Shiraz, Zinfandel, Merlot, Muscat, Chardonnay, Gewurtztraminer

Wine Types: table and dessert wines

Wine Procurement: Eagle Ranch gift shop and at Kelly Liquors in Albuquerque

WINERY FACILITIES:

Tasting Room: Yes

Meeting Room: Yes

Picnic Site: RV friendly

Restrooms: Yes

Snacks: small coffee shop serving pistachio ice cream and cappuccino

Lodgings: in Alamogordo and Tularosa

For information on Glassware and Tasting, Wine Service and Cooking with Wine, and Wine Storage, see appendix Wine ABCs beginning on page 110.

ZONE 2

Central Region

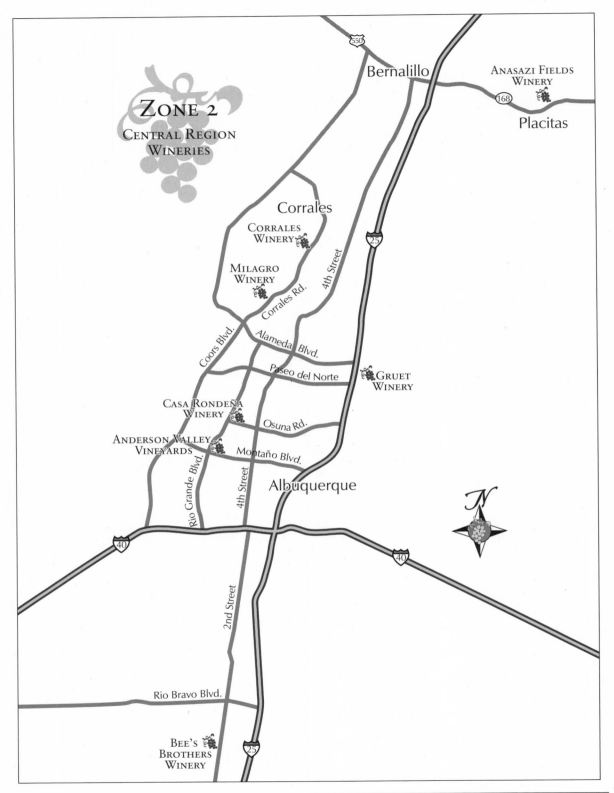

Zone 2
Central Region
Wineries

Bernalillo

Anasazi Fields
Winery

168

Placitas

Corrales

Corrales
Winery

Milagro
Winery

4th Street

25

Corrales Rd.

Coors Blvd.

Alameda Blvd.

Paseo del Norte

Gruet
Winery

Casa Rondeña
Winery

Osuna Rd.

Anderson Valley
Vineyards

Montaño Blvd.

Rio Grande Blvd.

4th Street

Albuquerque

N

40

40

2nd Street

Rio Bravo Blvd.

52

Bee's
Brothers
Winery

25

ZONE 2
CENTRAL REGION WINERIES
OF NEW MEXICO

Area from Belen north of I-40 to just south of
Jemez Springs and east to Ponderosa

VICINITY OF:
paved roads to winery
from nearest vicinity.

DISTANCES TO:
Miles to Vicinity

	Albuquerque	Farmington	Las Cruces	Clayton	Hobbs
Albuquerque	—	182	223	273	315
Anderson Valley Vineyards					
Bee's Brothers Winery					
Casa Rondeña Winery					
Gruet Winery					
Corrales	10	172	233	263	325
Corrales Winery					
Milagro Winery					
Bernalillo	15	166	238	273	333
Anasazi Fields Winery (in Placitas)					

53

San Felipe de Neri Church, Albuquerque, New Mexico.

54

Albuquerque

There are six wineries in the vicinity of Albuquerque: Anderson Valley Vineyards, Casa Rondeña Winery, Bees Brothers Winery, and Gruet Winery (in Albuquerque), and Milagro Winery and Corrales Winery (both in Corrales).

Albuquerque is New Mexico's largest city, containing approximately one-third of the state's population. It was founded in 1706 by New Mexico Governor Francisco Cuervo y Valdes. It began as a small Spanish settlement of the Rio Abajo, or lower river district, with its traditional plaza and a church surrounded by adobe houses. The original church, San Felipe de Neri, is still in use today. It is the oldest church in Albuquerque and has continuously served the community without interruption since 1706. It was originally founded and served by the Franciscan friars. After 1850, New Mexico became a part of the United States and Archbishop Lamy, a French-born priest and then head of the Catholic Church in the territory, invited Italian Jesuits to Albuquerque. They planted grape cuttings in Old Town, Albuquerque. The Jesuits were followed by French vintners, creating an explosion of wine production. Farmers throughout the region around Albuquerque devoted much of their acreage to grape cultivation and more and more wineries were opened throughout the region. A great influx of vintners from Europe immigrated to the area, bringing with them their winemaking skills.

Visitors from all over the country stop to see Albuquerque's gardens and architecture and to shop in old adobe buildings for Native American art, jewelry, crafts, and New Mexican cuisine. Old Town is the oldest of the neighborhoods and one of the most visited attractions.

It has maintained its distinct personality, embracing three cultures: Indian, Spanish, and Anglo. To insure its sense of tradition and charm, a zoning ordinance was enacted in the late 1940s to preserve its appearance. Apparent everywhere in Old Town is the Native American influence, especially in the food, crafts, and clothing.

When the Atchison, Topeka and Santa Fe Railroad arrived in Albuquerque in April of 1880, in order to avoid what is now Old Town, they laid the track east of the town and the Rio Grande. A new Albuquerque then grew up around the railroad station and there emerged two towns, the original one, now called Old Town, and the new town of Albuquerque. Albuquerque is still a fast-growing city. Its population is about a half million. At an elevation of fifty-four hundred feet, it has all the conveniences of any large city. It is a tourist's delight. It is conveniently situated near modern freeways and has become famous for its tram lift, the longest aerial tramway in the world, stretching 2.7 miles and rising thirty-seven hundred feet from the base of the mountain to the top, Sandia Peak, where there is a restaurant and a ski area. The imposing grandeur of the Sandia Mountains is spectacular from morning to sunset, as light and shadows play across its rock face, crosshatched with side canyons, changing its moods. They provide the perfect backdrop for the largest city in the Land of Enchantment: New Mexico.

55

Entrance to Anderson Valley Vineyards, Albuquerque, New Mexico.

ANDERSON VALLEY
VINEYARDS

You will know you're there when you see the large oak barrel that marks the entrance of this famous producer of fine wines. Anderson Valley Vineyards is nestled in the verdant fields of the northern Rio Grande Valley. It was founded by Maxie Anderson and his wife, Patty. Maxie Anderson was an ardent hot-air-balloon pilot. In 1975 he and his teammates, Ben Abruzzo and Larry Newman, made the first trans-Atlantic helium-balloon flight in the Double Eagle 2. In 1983 he perished in a balloon accident in West Germany.

After the tragic accident, his wife, Patty, and son, Kris, turned the winemaking hobby into a commercial venture. They converted their balloon-making building into a winery, applied for a commercial winemaking license, and were bonded in 1984. They performed their first commercial crush the same year. Since then, their award-winning wines have established them as one of the leaders of New Mexico wineries.

Anderson Valley Vineyards are known for their award-winning Chardonnay and Cabernets. The Balloon Blush is their signature wine. There are eight acres in production, and they also buy some grapes from Truth or Consequences and some from Colorado. They crush eighty to one hundred tons annually, producing about five to six thousand cases. During the Albuquerque International Balloon Fiesta, about thirty to three hundred visitors to the Anderson property are entertained. Events include special balloon launches. Private mass ascensions take off from the vineyards to pay homage to Maxie, and in the spring—weather permitting—there is a private after-glow Jazz Festival. The chief winemaker is Mark Matheson.

56

Oak barrels are used for their Cabernet Sauvignon, Chardonnay, Merlot, and Sauvignon Blanc. Anderson Valley wines can be purchased at almost every supermarket in New Mexico, Walgreens, all liquor stores, a number of restaurants in Albuquerque, and a few in Santa Fe. Along with their beautiful tasting room, their meeting room can accommodate one hundred people. For more information on facilities and accommodations, see the facing page.

DIRECTIONS FROM ALBUQUERQUE:

Take Rio Grande Blvd. north from I-40. Continue north past Montaño and the Montaño bridge. Look for the large barrel on the east side of the road. This barrel marks the entrance to the Anderson Valley Vineyards and Winery at 4920 Rio Grande Blvd. NW.

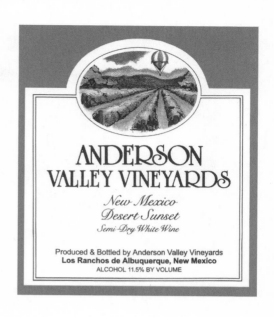

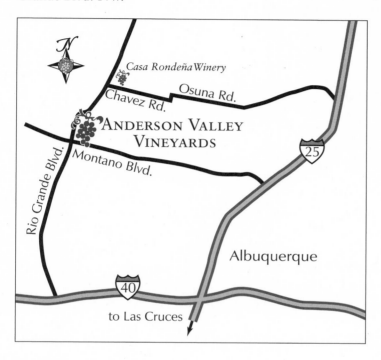

WINERY DETAILS:

Acres in Production: 8 on-site

Elevation: 5,000 feet

Hours: Noon–5 P.M. Tues.–Sun. most of the year. (Call to confirm.)

Proprietor: Patty Anderson

Distance from Albuquerque: within Albuquerque city limits

Location: north Rio Grande Blvd.

Mailing Address: 4920 Rio Grande Blvd. NW, Albuquerque, NM 87107

Telephone: (505) 344-7266

Founded: in 1973 by Patty and Maxie Anderson of hot-air balloon fame

Grape Varietals: Chardonnay, Cabernet Sauvignon, Sauvignon Blanc, Muscat, Merlot

Wine Types: table wines (reds, whites, and pinks, or rosés)

Wine Procurement: chain supermarkets, liquor stores, and many restaurants in Albuquerque and Santa Fe

WINERY FACILITIES:

Tasting Room: Yes

Meeting Room: accommodates 100 visitors

Picnic Site: Yes

Restrooms: Yes

Snacks: No

Lodgings: In Albuquerque

For information on Glassware and Tasting, Wine Service and Cooking with Wine, and Wine Storage, see appendix Wine ABCs beginning on page 110.

57

*The fermentation room at
Bee's Brothers Winery*

BEE'S BROTHERS WINERY

Although it is the smallest winery in the state it is probably the most unusual. It is the Bee's Brothers Winery, founded in the year 2000. Its wine is not made from grapes or fruit—it is made from a mixture of honey and water. The resulting wine is called *mead*. Historically, mead is one of the oldest wines in existence. One of the reasons mead was developed was that in countries that could not grow grapes, the viable alternative was mead. Since bees are hardy and thrive in most climates, they can be raised in almost any region of the world. They can survive in frosts and extremes of heat and cold.

The oldest meaderies in the world are in Poland (one is very famous). Another famous meadery is in Ireland, and another is in Scotland. Presently there are thirty-five meaderies in the United States. There are four or five in California, some are located in Oregon, and some are on the east coast. Bee's Brothers is the only one in New Mexico.

Owner Bill Smith started out as a beekeeper. He has had bees at different times throughout his life. His passion for bees and beekeeping was so apparent that it prompted his wife to give him a beehive for their wedding anniversary. "That's the way it started," Bill said, "I went from one hive to fifteen hives. This was eight years ago and as they do, one hive becomes two, two becomes four, four becomes six. It just happens that way—naturally—so pretty soon we had a lot of hives and a lot of honey. We began experimenting with diluted honey with water and making mead. We use about three pounds of honey to make a gallon of solution, then with the combination of yeast and nutrients, it ferments like any other kind of wine." Bill Smith learned his techniques in mead production by trial and error. He researched and read just about everything he could find on the subject. Presently he is using about three thousand pounds of honey and is producing three hundred cases. Mead's taste is pleasurably different— smooth and refreshing—with a rich honey taste that is carried over into all of their four varieties. A popular favorite is their Sweet Mead, a semi-sweet wine minus flavoring and spices. It is light, refreshing, and served chilled. It goes well with New Mexico cuisine, hot or spicy dishes, and ham.

Because the meadery is located in a residential district, visiting is not encouraged, but visitors may be invited on a limited basis by appointment only. See the facing page for wine procurement and availability of their four labels.

58

DIRECTIONS FROM ALBUQUERQUE:

Take I-25 south to Rio Bravo Blvd. Turn right (west) on Rio Bravo Blvd. Turn left on 2nd St. (south), then turn right (west) on Valley High, then left (south) on Community Lane. Turn right (west) on Nowicki Lane and continue to the winery at 619 Nowicki Lane.

WINERY DETAILS:

Acres in Production: not applicable; mead is made from honey

Elevation: 5,000 feet

Hours: *by appointment only*

Proprietor: Bill Smith

Distance from Albuquerque: in Albuquerque

Location: 619 Nowicki Lane SW

Mailing Address: 619 Nowicki Lane SW, Albuquerque, NM 87105

Telephone: (505) 452-3191

Fax: (505) 452-3192

E-mail: smith619@spinn.net

Website: www.beesbrothers.com

Founded: 2000 by Rick Hogan and Bill Smith

Grape Varietals: N/A; made from honey

Wine Types: table and dessert

Wine Procurement: Quarters, Jubilation Fine Wines, Kelly Liquors, John Brooks Foodtown, Liquor Barn, Cliffs Liquors, and Whole Foods in Santa Fe

WINERY FACILITIES:

Tasting Room: No

Meeting Room: No

Picnic Site: No

Restrooms: No

Snacks: No

Lodging: No

For information on Glassware and Tasting, Wine Service and Cooking with Wine, and Wine Storage, see appendix Wine ABCs beginning on page 110.

*Casa Rondeña Winery,
Albuquerque, New Mexico.*

CASA RONDEÑA WINERY

Casa Rondeña Winery is one of the most unique and beautifully styled wineries in New Mexico. It is located in the village of Los Ranchos de Albuquerque in the heart of the Rio Grande Valley. Casa Rondeña's winemaker, John Calvin, is a passionate wine historian who has an emotional attachment to the land near where he was born, in Los Ranchos de Albuquerque. His winemaking is an outgrowth of an appreciation for the agriculture-based economy of Albuquerque's early inhabitants in what is the oldest wine-producing region of the country. His time studying music in Spain exposed him to winemaking as well as to the music that is part of a broader cultural appreciation. The winemaker brings to his handcrafted wines a philosophy of treating wine as food and as a complement to good health. In his wine production, John continues to focus on quality rather than quantity.

Casa Rondeña Winery, making fine wines since 1995, welcomes visitors to their charming tasting room in one of several winery buildings exhibiting the Andalusian, southern Mediterranean style of architecture for which John and the winery are so well recognized. Either before or after tasting their fine wines, they invite visitors to stroll through the fermentation room and around the grounds alongside the vineyard and perhaps enjoy a glass or bottle of wine under the portal. Visitors strolling alongside the vineyard will note the Arabic influence in the arches of the windows and the green tile often used in southern Spain and northern Africa, particularly Morocco. From the front of the tasting room they will note the stone arches over the second-story windows, which are sandstone from northwestern India and are four to five hundred years old. The other grillwork is hand-carved sandstone that John designed and had made in India.

Casa Rondeña wines have won many awards, including *Best of Show* for their *Serenade* at the 2002 New Mexico Wine Competition. The Meritage and Cabernet Franc received awards at the Jerry Mead New World International Wine Competition. Their Cabernet Franc has received the top-rating score of all New Mexico red wines by the *Wine Spectator*. *USA Today* recognized Casa Rondeña as one of two top wineries in New Mexico. (The other is Gruet. See page 62.) *Hugh Johnson's Pocket Guide to Wine* gives three stars out of their international four-star rating to only Casa Rondeña and one other New Mexico winery.

Casa Rondeña award-winning wines include Cabernet Franc, Sangiovese, Meritage, Riesling, Sauvignon Blanc, Serenade, and Gewurztraminer.

60

DIRECTIONS FROM ALBUQUERQUE:

From I-25 go west on Osuna Road Turn left (south) on 4th St., then immediately right (left) on Chavez Road. It is a short distance to the winery at 733 Chavez Road.

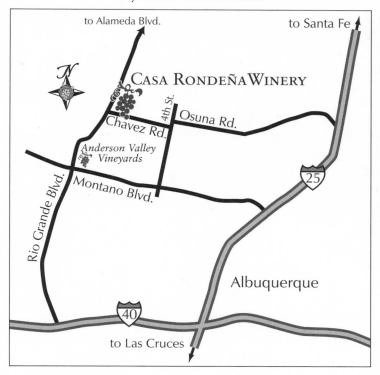

WINERY DETAILS:

Acres in Production: 5

Elevation: 5,280 feet

Hours: Wed.–Sat. 10 A.M. to 6 P.M., Sun. noon to 6 P.M.

Proprietor: John Calvin

Distance from Albuquerque: in North Valley of Albuquerque

Location: 733 Chavez Road

Mailing Address: 733 Chavez Road, Los Ranchos de Albuquerque, NM 87107

Telephone: (505) 344-5911 or (800) 706-1699

E-mail: info@casarondena.com

Website: www.casarondena.com

Founded: 1965

Grape Varietals: Cabernet Franc, Cabernet Sauvignon, Chardonnay, Riesling, Sauvignon Blanc, Gewurtztraminer

Wine Types: table, dessert, and sparkling wine

Wine Procurement: Restaurants in Albuquerque and Santa Fe, many supermarkets, and liquor stores. At Kelly Liquors, Sunflower, Costco, and Cost Plus

WINERY FACILITIES:

Tasting Room: Yes

Meeting Room: Yes

Picnic Site: Yes

Restrooms: Yes

Snacks: No

Lodgings: Close by

For information on Glassware and Tasting, Wine Service and Cooking with Wine, and Wine Storage, see appendix Wine ABCs beginning on page 110.

61

*Gruet Winery,
Albuquerque,
New Mexico.*

GRUET WINERY

The Gruet Winery originated in the champagne region of France, where the Gruet family founded its first champagne house and vineyards in 1952. Gilbert Gruet, the founder of Gruet Champagne, was the first to plant vineyards in Bethan (Marne), twenty miles south of Epernay, known for its excellent Chardonnay grapes. From its beginnings of bottling four hundred cases in the mid-1950s, Gilbert Gruet began the development of his vineyard and winery. He now produces one million bottles per year of Gruet Champagne in France.

Expansion in France offered limited opportunities, so the family sought to establish a second winery. They began to explore opportunities in the United States. In 1981 they came to California, and then the Southwest. Careful research proved that New Mexico's climate conditions of warm days and cool nights provided an ideal location for growing grapes. In 1984, Laurent Gruet, Farid Himeur, and Nathalie Gruet settled in New Mexico, bringing with them years of combined experience and expertise in the tradition of quality champagne production. In 1987 their first harvest from their vineyard in Truth or Consequences in southern New Mexico was ready.

They grow Chardonnay and Pinot Noir grapes in their own vineyards, but also purchase grapes from other growers. Their vineyards consist of 120 acres in production and produce about eighty thousand cases annually. The winery is located in Albuquerque and Laurent Gruet is the chief winemaker. His experience goes back to an early age, learning his skill in winemaking from his family's operation in France using the *Methode Champenoise* technique in production of their award-winning sparkling wines (their signature wines). They finish their Chardonnay and Pinot Noir grapes in French oak barrels, resulting in high-quality sparkling wines that have won many gold and silver medals since their first production. Gruet also produces award-winning still wines, using both Chardonnay and Pinot Noir varietals. Their wines can be purchased at liquor stores and supermarkets and are distributed and sold in forty-five states. See the facing page for more detailed information on visiting hours and facilities.

62

DIRECTIONS FROM ALBUQUERQUE:

The winery is located on the Pan American Freeway (I-25 frontage road) heading north just past Paseo del Norte (see map). The winery building is visible from I-25.

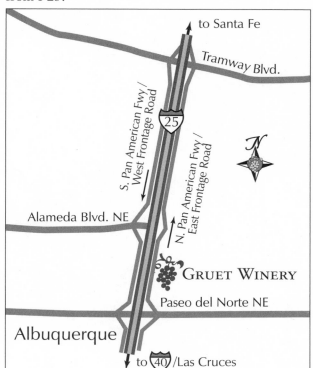

WINERY DETAILS:

Acres in Production: 120

Elevation: 5,000 feet

Hours: Mon.–Fri. 10 A.M.–5 P.M., Sat. noon–5 P.M., tours at 2 P.M.

Proprietor: Laurent and Nathalie Gruet, and Farid Himeur

Distance from Albuquerque: in Albuquerque

Location: off Pan American and Paseo del Norte

Mailing Address: 8400 Pan American NE, Albuquerque, NM 87113

Telephone: (505) 821-0055 or (888) 857-WINE

Fax: (505) 857-0066

E-mail: info@gruetwinery.com

Website: www.gruetwinery.com

Founded: 1984

Grape Varietals: Chardonnay, Pinot Noir

Wine Types: sparkling wine, red and white table wines

Wine Procurement: liquor stores and supermarkets; sold in 45 states

WINERY FACILITIES:

Tasting Room: Yes

Meeting Room: No

Picnic Site: No

Restrooms: Yes

Snacks: No

Lodgings: In town

For information on Glassware and Tasting, Wine Service and Cooking with Wine, and Wine Storage, see appendix Wine ABCs beginning on page 110.

63

Old San Ysidro Church, Corrales, New Mexico.

64

Corrales

There are two wineries in the vicinity of Corrales, Milagro Winery and Corrales Winery.

The Village of Corrales is an agricultural community, sitting at an elevation of 5,010 feet above sea level in a valley within the Rio Grande Rift, with the Sandia Mountains to the east and sandhill terraces to the west. The name *Corrales* is derived from the many corrals built along the river. Corrales occupies the eastern portion of the former Alameda Land Grant of 1710 , which was a parcel of land granted by the governor of the settlement to a retired corporal, Montes y Vigil. Captain Juan Gonzales bought the land in 1712.

The system of ditches, or acequias, is an important part of Corrales history. There is evidence that these acequias date back to ancient Pueblo people before the early Hispanic settlers adapted some of these ditches for their own use. Using this concept, Captain Gonzales dug a large ditch to provide water for irrigation of the farms and fields of the two communities along the Rio Grande. On the northern side of the ditch, the village was called Santa Rosalie de Corrales (Upper Corrales), the southern community, San Ysidro Corrales (Lower Corrales).

The "spine" of the community is Corrales Road, which starts at the city limits at Alameda Road in Albuquerque. It is a two-lane, undivided road, approximately seven miles long. It is the main road for the village of Corrales on the western bank of the Rio Grande, which was occupied by the ancient Tiguex Indians long before the early Spanish settled in the area. The road winds through the narrow, fertile floodplain of the Middle Rio Grande Valley. Along either side of the road are pastures alive with sheep, goats, horses, and cattle, and farms of fruit orchards, grape vineyards, and vegetables—especially corn and chile. Also lining the road on both sides are stands offering seasonal produce and native crafts.

For nearly two centuries, the Rio Grande Valley Franciscan priests had successfully grown grapes for their sacramental wine. The Rio Grande climate was ideal for grape growing and the land was less expensive than the available acreage in Europe, whose vintners were in search of more land at a lower cost. Consequently wine producers from France and Italy were attracted to the region. These immigrants brought their centuries-old skills to the Rio Grande Valley, and many settled in Corrales, which soon became famous as a producer of some of the finest wines and brandy in the country.

After the arrival of the Santa Fe Railroad in 1880, tourists from the east poured into Corrales and Albuquerque, and Corrales especially became a haven for artists, writers, sculptors, and "free-spirited" types. After its incorporation in 1972, its population more than doubled. Corrales is now a multicultural mix of people from around the world. A mixture of Old Spanish homesteads and modern adobes, unpaved rural lanes, galleries, and historical attractions such as the Old Historic San Ysidro Church built in 1868, offer visitors a journey into the past. As my good friend and popular mayor of Corrales, Gary Kanin, says, "What makes Corrales special is the fact that we have a distinct character of our own. We are trying to maintain that rural character as much as we possibly can, while supporting a great ethnic and economic mix. Corrales is still a place where you can stretch out, relax, and smell the roses."

65

Corrales Winery,
Corrales, New Mexico.

CORRALES WINERY

The Corrales Winery is located in the small agricultural village of Corrales, sitting at an elevation of 5,010 feet above sea level. Keith Johnstone, a retired engineer with a Ph.D. in engineering, and his wife, Barbara, founded it in the year 2000. Many years before opening the winery in 2001, Keith and Barbara were growing grapes and selling them to wineries. As it happened, every winery that they sold their grapes to was receiving gold medals for the wines that they produced from Keith's grapes. Keith and Barbara accepted the fact that *you can't make great wines from inferior grapes*, so they started their own winery. They presently have one acre of vines in production, which they will expand to four and a quarter acres. Barbara and Keith don't grow all of the grapes used in their wine production; they buy some from other growers in New Mexico (none from out of state). They buy from growers in Deming and northern New Mexico, and from a number of their neighbors who also grow grapes in the small village of Corrales. In 2003, they crushed about thirty tons of grapes, which produced about 2,000 to 2,500 cases. This is a combined effort of Keith and Barbara. They have no assistants, but use people on a seasonal basis to help with the pruning and harvesting. According to Keith, the weather has not been a factor in their successful yield of grapes. In fact, Keith says, "the dryer it is the better, as there is less chance of mildew." All of their plants are drip-irrigated, giving them control of the water from their own irrigation system, which is not dependent on the community wells. Keith is the chief winemaker. After an intensive study for a period of several years, with different types of oak and different toast barrels, Keith found that oak barrels were the best choice for the kind of wines he wanted to make from the kind of grapes grown in New Mexico. At present, the procurement of their wines is limited to festival sales and sales at the winery. Right now some of the wines produced are already sold, even before bottling, so the need for wholesalers to sell to commercial outlets is well into the future.

The Corrales Winery considers their Muscat Canelli, from the Muscat grapes grown in their own vineyard, their signature wine. They make it in a sweet preserve style that has a wonderful peach, apricot, pear, and honey flavor. Their red wines, like their popular Cabernet Franc and Cabernet Sauvignons, have all been silver- and gold-medal winners at the State Fair, which possibly accounts for the long waiting list for the wines to get bottled. See the facing page for more detailed information on the winery's facilities and accommodations for visitors.

66

DIRECTIONS FROM ALBUQUERQUE:

From Albuquerque take I-25 north to Exit 233, Alameda Blvd. Take Alameda Blvd. west, across the river. From Alameda Blvd. go north (right) on Corrales Road. It is about 4.5 miles north to Orchard Lane. Corrales Winery is just ahead at 6275 Corrales Rd.

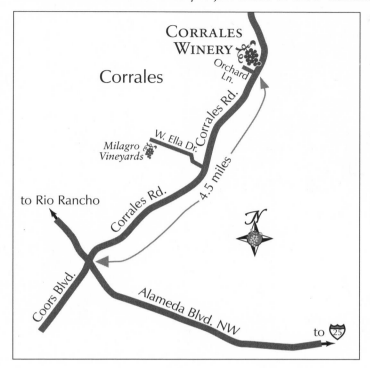

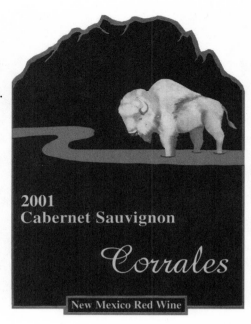

WINERY DETAILS:

Acres in Production: 1 to 4
Elevation: 5,000 feet
Hours: Wed.–Sun. noon–5 P.M.
Proprietor: Keith and Barbara Johnstone
Distance from Albuquerque: approximately 5 miles
Location: 6275 Corrales Rd.
Mailing Address: PO Box 527, Corrales, NM 87048
Telephone: (505) 898-5165
Fax: (505) 898-1819
E-mail: info@corraleswinery.com
Website: www.corraleswinery.com
Founded: September 2000
Grape Varietals: Muscat Canelli, Cabernet Sauvignon, Cabernet Franc
Wine Types: red and white table, dessert, and proprietary blends
Wine Procurement: at festivals and at the winery

WINERY FACILITIES:

Tasting Room: Yes
Meeting Room: No
Picnic Site: Yes
Restrooms: Yes
Snacks: No
Lodgings: In village

For information on Glassware and Tasting, Wine Service and Cooking with Wine, and Wine Storage, see appendix Wine ABCs beginning on page 110.

67

*Milagro Winery,
Corrales, New Mexico.*

MILAGRO
VINEYARDS & WINERY

The Milagro Winery is a small winery in the picturesque agricultural village of Corrales, where early Spanish, French, and Italian settlers planted their vineyards in the rich bottomland soil by the river. Time has not changed its European character and old-world charm, nor has it changed in its production of fine grapes for winemaking, as practiced by the early Franciscan friars who produced small quantities of wine for their sacraments. The Milagro Winery, whose owners, Rick and Mitzi Hobson, have been growing grapes since 1985, carries on this traditional, hands-on practice of producing small amounts of quality wine.

They founded the winery in 1999. They also buy grapes from other growers in the village and other growers in the state. The help of their neighbors and the Hobsons' reciprocal assistance has made possible the Hobsons' goal of making the finest wine, by using only the traditional vinifer wine grapes grown in New Mexico. Their total production last year was about one thousand cases, targeting for about two thousand cases this year. Rick is a chemical engineer and the chief winemaker. His winemaking skills are self-taught and have been honed over the years by intensive reading and research, gleaning techniques from knowledgeable vintners, and by taking courses in oenology from the University of California at Davis. In the past four years the Hobsons have not used pesticides in the vineyard, and if they choose, they are qualified to become a certified organic grower.

The winery uses mostly French oak and some American oak for processing their red table wines. Their wines can be purchased at the winery and at stores and restaurants in Albuquerque, Bernalillo, and Santa Fe.

68

Milagro specializes in Merlot, Chardonnay, and Zinfandels. These are the three grape varietals that seem to thrive the best on the Milagro property. They produce two outstanding table wines—Corrales Red and Corrales White—and a very fine Zinfandel. They also bottle a Chardonnay, a Merlot, and a Sauvignon, all sold under the Milagro label. For detailed information on Milagro's visiting hours and accommodations, see the facing page.

DIRECTIONS FROM ALBUQUERQUE:

From Albuquerque take I-25 north to Exit 233, Alameda Blvd. Take Alameda Blvd. west, across the river. From Alameda Blvd. go north (right) on Corrales Road for 2.4 miles (until you see the Wells Fargo Bank on your left). Take the next left, West Ella, and go 1 mile to the winery at 985 West Ella.

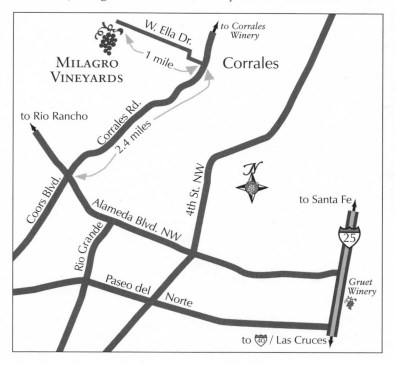

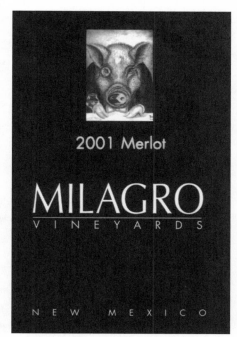

WINERY DETAILS:

Acres in Production: 10
Elevation: 5,000 feet
Hours: *by appointment only*
Proprietor: Rick and Mitzi Hobson
Mailing Address: PO Box 1205, Corrales, NM 87048
Distance from Albuquerque: 1 mile
Location: 985 West Ella
Telephone: (505) 898-3998
E-mail: contact@milagrovineyardsandwinery.com
Website: www.milagrovineyardsandwinery.com
Founded: winery in 1999, growing grapes since 1985
Grape Varietals: Zinfandel, Merlot, Chardonnay, Cabernets
Wine Types: table
Wine Procurement: at winery, P. F. Chang's, Zinc Wine Bar and Bistro, Quarters, Range Café and Gift Shop in Bernalillo, Liquor Barn in Santa Fe

WINERY FACILITIES:

Tasting Room: Yes
Meeting Room: No
Picnic Site: No
Restrooms: Yes
Snacks: No
Lodgings: In town

For information on Glassware and Tasting, Wine Service and Cooking with Wine, and Wine Storage, see appendix Wine ABCs beginning on page 110.

Our Lady of Sorrows Church, Bernalillo, New Mexico.

70

Bernalillo / Placitas

There is one winery in the vicinity of Bernalillo. It is Anasazi Fields Winery, located in the small village of Placitas just two miles east of the town of Bernalillo.

Bernalillo is a town with a population of approximately thirty-seven hundred, located eighteen miles north of Albuquerque off I-25. Long before the conquistadors settled in the area, Bernalillo was the site of prehistoric Tiguex Pueblos. As early as the mid-1600s, the Spanish settlers built their haciendas and adobe huts along the river. The largest hacienda was built by the Gonzales-Bernal family. At that time Bernalillo was known as Little Bernal. The settlers remained in Little Bernal until the Pueblo Revolt in 1680, led by Popé, a militant Indian leader who forced them to flee and return to Mexico. The settlers returned in 1682 after another Spanish conquest.

During their conquest, then governor Don Diego de Vargas founded the town of Bernalillo in 1695. The town grew rapidly, thrived, and became an important trading center consisting of twenty-seven families. A local tradesman, Nathan Bibbo, established the Bernalillo Mercantile Company, a huge inventory of every possible need for the community, stocking everything from native herbs, clothing, harnesses, and coffins to cookstoves, hardware, building materials, tools, and hundreds of other items needed for the home, ranch, and farm.

With the coming of the Santa Fe Railroad in the late 1880s, the main track passed through the center of town. The town leaders tried to negotiate with José Leandro Perea, the town's largest landowner, for purchase of more land to build shops and yards for the railroad, but Perea priced the land so high that the railroad negotiators went twenty miles south to Albuquerque for better terms, thereby depriving Bernalillo of a great opportunity to become a great city. Although Bernalillo has developed into a prosperous community with restaurants, fine accommodations, and services for tourists (including a popular Indian casino), the dominant population is Hispanic and many still observe Spanish culture and customs dating back more than two centuries.

Just two miles to the east of Bernalillo, at the I-25 interchange that connects with NM 165, is the small village of Placitas, which was built on the site of an ancient Indian Pueblo. It is a village with a shopping center and large homes, populated by many who seek the quiet life away from crowded, large cities. Just beyond this community is the home of the Anasazi Fields Winery detailed on page 72.

71

Anasazi Fields Winery fermenting tanks, Placitas, New Mexico.

ANASAZI FIELDS WINERY

The Anasazi Fields Winery sits on the western edge of the old village of Placitas, surrounded by orchards and watered by a spring-fed irrigation system that dates back more than a thousand years to a time when the Anasazi people farmed the Placitas Valley. The winery is built in the old hacienda style. New facilities have recently been added to make Anasazi Fields one of the most hospitable places to taste wine and enjoy an afternoon, either on a visit or during the special events held seasonally. Anasazi Fields Winery was founded in 1993 by Jim Fish and three friends who incorporated that year and turned a hobby into a small commercial winery. It was opened to the public in 1995. Today, the corporation consists of thirty-one partners and ten thousand gallons of wine aging in their cellar. They are steadily increasing sales and growing a reputation as the leading producer of fine, dry table wines made from fruits and berries. They do not use grapes. They produce both red and white fruit wines from fruit grown in their own orchards. They grow about one third of the fruit and the rest is purchased from other New Mexico growers. These fine, dry wines are oak-aged for two to three years before bottling. Fruits used include raspberry, apricot, peach, apple, plum, blackberry, and cranberry. A popular wine club is available for convenient access to these unusual wines as well as a cookbook for pairing them with food.

Vintner Jim Fish and his thirty-one partners have eight acres in production and crush twenty to thirty tons of fruit a year, which results in about 1,500 to 2,000 cases annually. Jim Fish is the principal owner and chief winemaker. He has a Ph.D. in chemical engineering. Dana Army is his assistant and a half dozen other people assist in the operation. They also have a Ph.D. biologist involved in the operation.

The Anasazi Fields wines can be purchased at the winery and are available at all the large wine shops in Santa Fe and Albuquerque. One of their signature wines is an apricot dry white wine—light, crisp, and refreshing. For more information on Anasazi Field's facilities, visiting hours, and accommodations, see the facing page.

DIRECTIONS FROM ALBUQUERQUE:

From Albuquerque take I-25 north to Bernalillo (16 miles), then take exit 242, turn right (east), and go 6.2 miles to the small village of Placitas. Follow the signs to the winery.

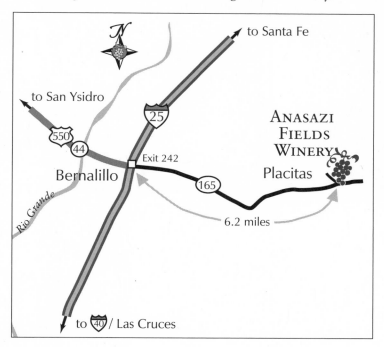

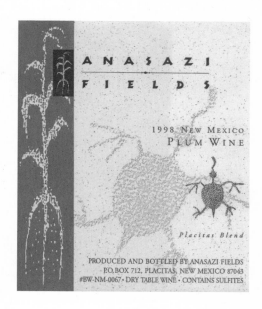

WINERY DETAILS:

Acres in Production: 8

Elevation: 6,000 feet

Hours: Wed.–Sun. noon–5 P.M.

Proprietor: Jim Fish and 31 partners

Distance from Albuquerque: 18 miles

Location: 26 Camino de las Pueblitas
(on the western edge of Placitas)

Mailing Address: PO Box 712, Placitas, NM 87043

Telephone: (505) 867-3062

E-mail: anasazifieldswinery@att.net

Website: www.anasazifieldswinery.com

Founded: 1993

Grape Varietals: No grapes used. Wines are made
from fruit only

Wine Types: dry white and red table wine made from
apricots, plums, apples, peaches, cherries, cranberries,
blackberries, strawberries, and raspberries

Wine Procurement: at the winery and at all large wine
shops in Santa Fe and Albuquerque

WINERY FACILITIES:

Tasting Room: Yes

Meeting Room: Yes

Picnic Site: Yes

Restrooms: Yes

Snacks: No

Lodgings: In town of Bernalillo

*For information on Glassware and
Tasting, Wine Service and Cooking
with Wine, and Wine Storage, see
appendix Wine ABCs beginning
on page 110.*

ZONE 3

Northern Region

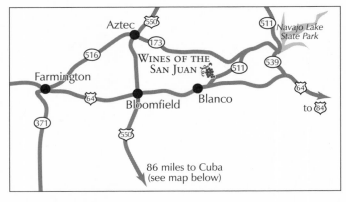

Aztec — 550 — 173
516
Farmington
WINES OF THE
SAN JUAN
64
371
Bloomfield — Blanco — 511 — 539
550
511 — Navajo Lake
State Park
64
to 84

86 miles to Cuba
(see map below)

ZONE 3
NORTHERN REGION
WINERIES

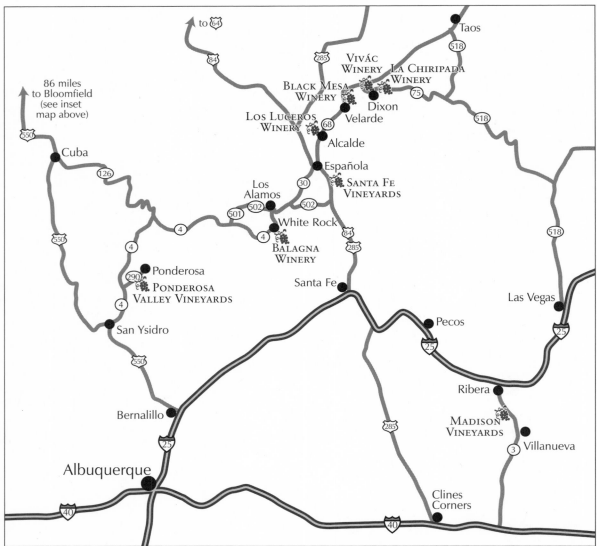

to 64

84

285

Taos

518

VIVÁC
WINERY

LA CHIRIPADA
WINERY

BLACK MESA
WINERY

75

518

DIXON

LOS LUCEROS
WINERY

68

Velarde

86 miles
to Bloomfield
(see inset
map above)

Alcalde

550

Cuba

Española

126

SANTA FE
VINEYARDS

30

Los
Alamos

502

502

501

White Rock

84

518

4

285

4

BALAGNA
WINERY

4

Ponderosa

290

Santa Fe

Las Vegas

PONDEROSA
VALLEY VINEYARDS

4

Pecos

San Ysidro

25

550

Ribera

Bernalillo

MADISON
VINEYARDS

285

25

3 Villanueva

76

Albuquerque

Clines
Corners

40

25

40

ZONE 3
NORTHERN REGION WINERIES OF NEW MEXICO

Area from Santa Fe and Las Vegas North to Dixon

VICINITY OF: *paved roads to winery* *from nearest vicinity.*	DISTANCES TO: *Miles to Vicinity*				
	Albuquerque	Farmington	Las Cruces	Clayton	Hobbs
Bloomfield / Blanco Wines of the San Juan	158	24	381	352	473
San Ysidro / Jemez Springs Ponderosa Valley Vineyards and Winery	41	141	284	273	315
Los Alamos Balagna Winery	93	193	318	228	342
Las Vegas	123	199	282	214	308
Ribera *(25 miles southwest of Las Vegas off I-25)* Madison Vineyards & Winery	104	224	269	125	360
Española Santa Fe Vineyards	84	174	307	333	309
Alcalde *(7 miles north of Española)* Los Luceros Winery	91	231	307	203	340
Velarde *(13 miles north of Española)* Black Mesa Winery	97	237	246	196	346
Dixon *(17 miles south of Taos)* La Chiripada Winery Vivac Winery	112	231	280	179	346

Navajo Lake, north of Blanco, New Mexico.

78

Bloomfield / Blanco

In the vicinity of Bloomfield there is one winery, the Wines of the San Juan, located in the town of Blanco (just nine miles east of Bloomfield).

Bloomfield is located on the San Juan River in northwestern New Mexico, at the junction of NM 44 and US 64. It has a population of sixty-five hundred and lies at an elevation of 5,395 feet above sea level. Bloomfield is a ranching and farming community situated in the center of an oil- and gas-producing region, whose industries provide many of the jobs and revenues for the community. Bloomfield had its beginnings in the late 1800s as a trading post set up by an army general whose name was Porter, after whom the town was originally named. Later the name was changed to Bloomfield. Bloomfield has known turbulent times. It was here that the infamous character from the Lincoln County War, Port Stockton, was hired as a peace officer, but his criminal ways led to his dismissal. He resumed his outlaw activities, terrorizing the town with stagecoach hold-ups, shootings, and cattle rustlings. Stockton was killed in 1881 by a sheriff hunting for a gun-slinger Stockton was hiding. The shootings and violence continued for some years until the lawlessness finally settled down, and Bloomfield became the trading center for farmers and ranchers in the area.

An interesting attraction in the Bloomfield area is the Salmon Ruins Archaeological Site and Museum, located just two miles west of Bloomfield on US 64. It is one of the largest of the Ancestral Puebloan villages built by people of Chaco Canyon in the eleventh century. Visitors can tour Salmon Ruins by trail and view the many artifacts recovered from the ruins on display in the adjacent museum. Bloomfield has adequate accommodations for tourists as well as grocery stores, restaurants, and service stations.

Just nine miles east of Bloomfield on US 64 is the town of Blanco, where the Wines of the San Juan is located. Visitors are welcome to visit the winery's rustic tasting room just north of the village on NM 511, six miles below the Navajo Lake State Park, where fishermen enjoy world-class, quality water fishing below the dam in the San Juan River. Wines of the San Juan is detailed on page 80.

79

Wines of the San Juan Tasting Room, photograph by Marcia Arnold.

WINES OF THE SAN JUAN

The Wines of the San Juan is a family business owned by Dave and Marcia Arnold, who had owned and operated a dairy farm in Wisconsin. After twenty years of operating their farm they decided to seek more profitable and interesting agri-opportunities elsewhere. They ceased operation of their farm and in 1993 moved to Colorado, where they managed an alfalfa farm. Noting the many flourishing vineyards in the Colorado area, they decided to explore the idea of growing grapes and making wine. After a visit with Henry Street, a successful grower and winemaker in northern New Mexico, and with his encouragement, they decided to find an ideal site to start a vineyard and winery.

They found the perfect site in the Four Corners area of New Mexico. It is nestled deep in the bosque along the San Juan River, just five minutes north of Blanco in the small village of Turley, only a few miles south of the Navajo Dam. This part of the San Juan River is considered the number-one trophy trout–fishing area in America, a fisherman's paradise attracting sportsmen the world over. Whether fly-fishing in the quality waters, vacationing, or out for a Sunday drive, visitors are welcome to stop at the Arnolds' rustic little tasting room to try some of their great wines.

Dave Arnold is the chief winemaker—his degree in biology and intensive study and experience in agriculture and winemaking more than qualifies him to be a successful vintner. The winery is a work in progress, becoming more family oriented. Their three children contribute to the physical labor and the technical needs of the operation. Their youngest daughter, Jennifer, just received her B.A. degree in agriculture from Fort Lewis College in Durango. Their son, Joshua, is the artist and label designer, and daughter Kim handles the computer research and setup. They are growing fifteen acres of grapes stretching along Highway 511 east of the entry gate. A crop of Chardonnay, Merlot, and Cabernets will be ready for crushing, processing, and bottling in 2005, and they are looking forward to producing about one thousand cases from the first year's harvest. Their signature wine is a Riesling named "Blue Winged Olive," after a popular fly known to anglers all over the west. Blue Winged Olive is their bestseller. They are presently bringing their wines in from Deming and some peach wines are offered when peaches are in season. Their wines are sold under the Wines of the San Juan label and can be purchased in Farmington liquor stores. For more details on visiting hours, facilities, and accommodations, see the facing page.

80

DIRECTIONS FROM ALBUQUERQUE:

Take I-25 north Exit 242 at Bernalillo. Go northwest on US 550 to Bloomfield, then go 9 miles east on US 64 to Blanco. Turn north on NM 511. It is about 6 miles to the tasting room at 233 Highway 511.

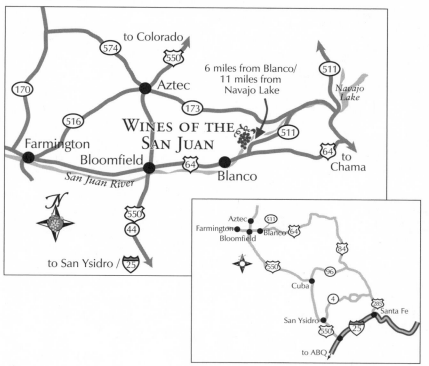

WINERY DETAILS:

Acres in Production: 15

Elevation: 5,600 feet

Hours: Mon.–Sat. 10 A.M.–6 P.M., Sun. noon–6 P.M.

Proprietor: David and Marcia Arnold

Distance from Albuquerque: 129 miles

Location: in Blanco about 11 miles southwest of Navajo Lake

Mailing Address: 233 Highway 511, Blanco, NM 87412

Telephone: (505) 632-0879

Fax: (505) 632-8709

E-mail: sales@winesofthesanjuan.com

Website: www.winesofthesanjuan.com

Founded: March 2003

Grape Varietals: Merlot, Chardonnay, Cabernet Sauvignon, Blanco Rosé, Gewurtztraminer, Muscat

Wine Types: table and fortified

Wine Procurement: Bluffs Package Liquor Store in Farmington, in a country club and a couple of restaurants in Aztec

WINERY FACILITIES:

Tasting Room: located 6 miles below Navajo State Park on Hwy 511

Meeting Room: porch can serve as a meeting room and can hold 12–20 people

Picnic Site: with tables

Restrooms: Yes

Snacks: No

Lodgings: in Bloomfield and in the small community of Navajo Dam

For information on Glassware and Tasting, Wine Service and Cooking with Wine, and Wine Storage, see appendix Wine ABCs beginning on page 110.

81

Via Coeli Monastery, Jemez Springs, New Mexico.

82

San Ysidro/Jemez Springs

In the vicinity of San Ysidro / Jemez Springs is one winery and vineyard, Ponderosa Valley Winery, an award-winning winery in the small village of Ponderosa in the Jemez Mountains.

Jemez Springs is located in the Jemez Mountains within an hour's drive from Albuquerque. It is an incorporated village, with a population of about five hundred, lying at an elevation of 6,400 above sea level. To get there from Albuquerque, take I-25 north to exit 242 (Farmington). Turn west onto NM 44 to San Ysidro, then right on NM 4, and go eighteen miles to Jemez Springs. The drive to Jemez Springs from San Ysidro is pleasant and colorful as you pass through a series of communities, small farms, and pasturelands. Along the way, one is momentarily surprised by a half-mile stretch of red rock formations, softly sculptured by the wind. A short distance north is Jemez Pueblo, which has been occupied continuously since 1696. Visitors are welcome in the pueblo, but permission to take pictures is required.

During the warm seasons of spring and summer, roadside stands are set up by the Indians from the pueblo to sell their tamales, fried bread, and round loaves of bread baked in outdoor ovens called *hornos*. Continuing north through Jemez Canyon (*el cañon de Don Diego*), many travelers pause at about four-fifths of a mile north of mile post 11 to see if they can spot the outline of a robed figure near the top of the cliff wall on the west side of the highway. The tale is told that long ago, while a band of besieged Indians were fighting off assailants from the top of the bluff, their patron saint, St. James, suddenly appeared. Their assailants made a fast retreat when they spotted the apparition. An image said to be that of St. James appears to be etched on the wall of the cliff below.

Jemez Springs is a vibrant community with a modern fire station, a police station, a community library, an arts and crafts club, and a medical clinic. Also available in emergencies is the Jemez Valley Medical System Inc., started in 1974 to develop teams of paramedics to cover the Jemez area.

Well worth visiting is the Via Coeli Monastery at the northern end of the village, famous for its beautiful gardens, art treasures, and its use as a retreat for Catholic priests. The Jemez State Monument, just across the road from the monastery, marks the ruins of the old Jemez Mission, built around 1617 under the direction of Spanish priests. It is one of the best examples of seventeenth-century Spanish mission architecture in this part of the country. A mile up the road is Soda Dam, an interesting stop for travelers. It is a natural formation of calcium carbonate deposits that formed a dam. The water in this area is highly mineralized—hot mineral springs are prevalent throughout the Jemez Mountains. And it is the deposits from these thermal springs that precipitate out to form the dam.

In and around Jemez Springs there are many recreational opportunities, which include excellent camping and picnic facilities, hunting, fishing, cross-country skiing, and hiking. Just four miles north of Soda Dam off NM 4 are five camping or picnic grounds, all within a two-mile stretch. Continue on for eighteen miles, and you will reach Fenton Lake. Four miles farther, off NM 126, you will reach Seven Springs Fish Hatchery and the Ic Pond.

83

Ponderosa Valley Winery and Tasting Room, Ponderosa, New Mexico.

PONDEROSA VALLEY
VINEYARDS & WINERY

A nuclear design engineer at Sandia National Laboratories turned winemaker is the unique background of Henry Street and his Ponderosa Valley Vineyards and Winery. This rugged outdoorsman, Henry Street, and his wife, Mary, bought some acreage in the scenic Ponderosa Valley located on the southern slope of the Jemez Mountains, east of the small village of San Ysidro. Henry and Mary's intention was to use the property as a camping retreat. The property is in the area where the Valdera family planted the first grapes in the valley in 1887. The lush vineyards aroused an interest in the small village. Vineyards quickly spread throughout the valley, as almost everyone began to grow grapes.

The preponderance of vineyards in the area aroused Henry's interest also. He began to ask questions and started to grow his own grapes as a "spare-time" hobby. Many grape varieties cannot thrive at Ponderosa's elevation of 5,909 feet, so Henry started researching viticulture techniques around the world. He also took courses in oenology at the University of California at Davis, and with experimentation, found that Rieslings and a clone of the Pinot Noir grapes were the most hardy and adaptable to the cold winter valley. He planted his first cuttings in 1976 and for three years after its first harvest, he sold to other wineries. In 1991, with the help of his son, he built a winery amidst the surrounding vineyards. The winery was opened in 1993, specializing in Estate-Bottled wine, using the same recognizable bottle design as used in the Estate-Bottled Burgundy wines of France. The Ponderosa Rieslings are processed in American oak barrels and the wines that they finish are consistent award winners. Henry Street is the largest producer of Rieslings in the state. He also produces a Pinot Noir and a Cabernet. To please other palates the Streets also produce an apple wine made from four varieties of New Mexico apples. This winery, surrounded by lush vineyards, has not only been producing award-winning Riesling, but provides a magnificent setting for a visit to its tasting room while spending a relaxed interval on the porch sipping a great wine.

For more information on wine procurement, visiting hours, and facilities see the facing page.

84

DIRECTIONS FROM ALBUQUERQUE:

Take I-25 north Exit 242 at Bernalillo. Go northwest on US 550 to San Ysidro. Turn right (north) on NM 4, go 3 miles to NM 290. Turn right and go 3.1 miles on to vineyard on the left at 3171 Highway 290.

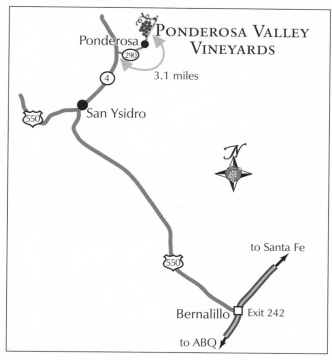

WINERY DETAILS:

Acres in Production: 8.5

Elevation: 5,909 feet

Hours: Tues.–Sat. 10 A.M.–5 P.M., Sun. noon–5 P.M.

Proprietor: Henry Street

Distance from Albuquerque: 45 miles

Location: in Ponderosa, a small village in the Jemez Mountains

Mailing Address: 3171 Highway 290, Ponderosa, NM 87044

Telephone: (505) 834-7487 or (800) WINEMKR

Fax: (505) 834-7073

E-mail: winemaker@ponderosawinery.com

Website: www.ponderosawinery.com

Founded: by Henry Street in 1993, first planting of grapes in 1976

Grape Varietals: Rieslings, Pinot Noir, Chardonnay, Cabernets, Blancs

Wine Types: red and white table wines

Wine Procurement: in retail liquor stores and supermarkets in Albuquerque, Socorro, Santa Fe, northern New Mexico, and Farmington

WINERY FACILITIES:

Tasting Room: Yes

Meeting Room: no group facilities

Picnic Site: on porch or under an arbor

Restrooms: Yes

Snacks: candy and soft drinks

Lodgings: in Jemez Springs about 15 miles north of Highways 4 and 290

For information on Glassware and Tasting, Wine Service and Cooking with Wine, and Wine Storage, see appendix Wine ABCs beginning on page 110.

85

Municipal building, Los Alamos, New Mexico.

86

Los Alamos / White Rock

There is one winery in the vicinity of Los Alamos / White Rock. The Balagna Winery's tasting room offers spectacular scenery, overlooking an eight-hundred-foot gorge of the Rio Grande.

Never did Ashley Pond, a Detroit businessman, dream when he founded the Los Alamos Ranch School for Boys in 1918 that twenty-five years later it would become the birthplace of the world's first atom bomb. The Los Alamos Ranch School was hidden on the eastern slope of the Jemez Mountains on the Pajarito Plateau, 7,300 feet above sea level, where boys studied the classics and hiked, fished, and rode horseback in the surrounding area.

In the closing months of 1942, during World War II, the United States conducted an extensive search for a location to establish a laboratory research site to produce an atomic bomb. Because of its highly secret nature, several requirements had to be met regarding its location. Isolation and an ideal year-round climate were the first priorities along with such factors as roads, railroads, ease of access to testing grounds, and available housing. The Los Alamos Ranch School met all requisites, so in 1942 it was chosen by the Manhattan District United States Corps of Engineers. The school's buildings were converted into laboratories, creating the secret "Atomic City," whose perimeters were guarded around the clock by men on horseback, uniformed patrols, and manned watchtowers.

After the mission was completed, and with the resulting defeat of Japan, politicians and scientists realized that the work that began during the war must be harnessed for peacetime use. Thus, the research installation expanded its interests and responsibilities and now devotes a large part of its efforts to the peaceful application of space exploration and atomic energy.

Today, Los Alamos is an incorporated city-county with two main residential and commercial areas: Los Alamos and White Rock. It is a community of twenty thousand people. There are deep canyons spanned by bridges and well-maintained roads, landscaped streets, and modern buildings and homes with well-kept lawns. Stands of ponderosa, piñon pine, and spruce blanket the mountains and mesas bordering the town. There are roads that snake through some of the most beautiful parts of the Santa Fe National Forest.

There is something for everyone in Los Alamos County. There are slopes for the skier whether beginner, intermediate, or expert. Cross-country skiing is available too, practically at one's doorstep. Excellent camping, fishing, hunting, picnicking, and hiking are available. Some of these recreational opportunities and their facilities are within the city limits. The recreational facilities include an eighteen-hole championship golf course, tennis courts, and swimming pools. There are many horseback-riding trails, playing fields for soccer, baseball, and softball for all ages. Also available are many civic, cultural, and arts activities. There are several shopping areas, and a wide variety of goods and services are available, all close to hotel accommodations and restaurants within town.

87

Balagna Winery Tasting Room, White Rock, New Mexico.

BALAGNA WINERY

The Balagna Winery is located on the edge of White Rock Canyon overlooking a gorge with a spectacular view of the Rio Grande hundreds of feet below. The proprietor and operator, John Balagna, started the winery in 1986 after his retirement from Los Alamos National Laboratory, ending a forty-year career there as a nuclear chemist. A background in chemistry is an important contributing factor to fine wine production and this knowledge is reflected in John Balagna's wines. His background and experience in winemaking goes back to his early growing-up years when he learned the art of winemaking from his grandfather, an immigrant from Italy in 1880 who employed the same winemaking skills he developed from his roots in the region of Piedmont, Italy. He passed them on to his grandson, John, who helped his grandfather make his wine. During Prohibition John's grandfather was making an everyday table wine, as many Italian immigrants did. The wine was called Dago Red. Today John's signature wine bears the same name, Dago Red—a smooth, red table wine and one of his best sellers, accounting for about one-third of his sales.

Because of the location's high altitude and harsh extremes in winter temperatures, John does not grow his own grapes, but buys all of his grapes from New Mexico growers, mostly from southern New Mexico. He produces about one thousand cases a year using stainless steel barrels and oak chips from oak-barrel builders in California. After the chips soak in the barrels for about a month, he tastes periodically and the chips are removed when the proper flavor is achieved. As John says, "My chemistry background helps to make a good wine, but cleanliness and good grapes are also required, and New Mexico grapes stack up well against any grown elsewhere." His other sources of grape supply are Rieslings from the Jemez Mountains, French hybrids and vinifers from south of Belen, and Zinfandels from vineyards in Alamogordo. Each of these areas is ideal for the development of good acid, sugar balance, and varietal flavors in the grapes. The Balagna Winery produces both single varietals and blends. Their signature wine is La Bomba Grande, a novelty wine released in 1993 to commemorate the fiftieth anniversary of the atom bomb. Its label depicts a mushroom cloud of the first A-Bomb test at Trinity Site in southern New Mexico in 1943. The wine received national publicity. It was featured in *Newsweek* and is now one of his best sellers. It is a blend of 50 percent Zinfandel, 25 percent Pinot Noir, and 25 percent Merlot.

John welcomes visitors to his attractive tasting room and urges visitors to bring a lunch and enjoy a taste of his wine on his outdoor portal. See the facing page for visiting hours and facilities.

88

Directions from Albuquerque:

From US 285 north of Santa Fe go west on NM 502, then take NM 4 to White Rock. Go south to Monte Rey Dr. North. Continue until it becomes Rio Bravo Drive. The winery is at 223 Rio Bravo Drive.

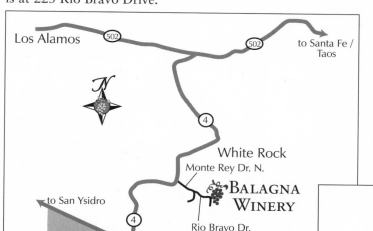

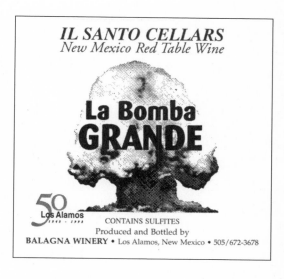

IL SANTO CELLARS
New Mexico Red Table Wine

La Bomba GRANDE

50 Los Alamos 1943–1993

CONTAINS SULFITES
Produced and Bottled by
BALAGNA WINERY • Los Alamos, New Mexico • 505/672-3678

Winery Details:

Acres in Production: None

Elevation: 7,000 feet

Hours: Tues.–Sun. noon–6 P.M. (closed Mon.)

Proprietor: John Balagna

Distance from Albuquerque: approximately 100 miles

Location: in White Rock, a small community adjacent to, and southwest of, Los Alamos

Mailing Address: 233 Rio Bravo Dr., Los Alamos (White Rock), NM 87544

Telephone: (505) 672-3678

Fax: (505) 672-1482

Founded: 1986

Grape Varietals: Zinfandels, Vidal Blanc, Chardonnay, Riesling, Barbera, Seyval Blanc, Chancellor, Merlot

Wine Types: table

Wine Procurement: two outlets in Los Alamos, one in White Rock, three in Santa Fe, and at winery

Winery Facilities:

Tasting Room: Yes

Meeting Room: Yes

Picnic Site: Yes

Restrooms: Yes

Snacks: No

Lodgings: at Hampton Inn in White Rock and in Los Alamos

For information on Glassware and Tasting, Wine Service and Cooking with Wine, and Wine Storage, see appendix Wine ABCs beginning on page 110.

89

Plaza Hotel, Las Vegas, New Mexico.

Las Vegas / Villanueva

There is one vineyard in the vicinity of Las Vegas. It is Madison Vineyards, located about twenty-five miles south of Las Vegas on a picturesque road off NM 3. From Albuquerque, NM 3 is reached by taking exit 323 off I-40 east. The highway follows the Pecos River between Villanueva and I-25. Villanueva lies six miles south of the winery.

Las Vegas is situated on the Old Santa Fe Trail in the foothills of the Sangre de Cristo Mountains. It lies at an elevation of 6,380 feet above sea level, with an Indo-Hispanic and Anglo population of about fifteen thousand. Las Vegas has a colorful history that dates back to 1835, when fifteen Spanish families received a grant from the Mexican government. They constructed a plaza, which soon became the center of life and a prosperous trading center, serving the merchants, traders, ranchers, wagon trains, and stagecoaches that traveled the Santa Fe Trail, which connected Independence, Missouri, with Santa Fe, California, and Mexico. Las Vegas was once the most prosperous and largest commercial center in the New Mexico Territory. Everywhere you go, the color, architecture, culture, and history of more than 150 years are evident. Dotting the dramatic scenery of the countryside and valleys around Las Vegas are old churches, chapels, historic buildings, and other architectural treasures, which lend a special charm to the city. Some nine hundred of these architectural treasures have been placed in the National Register of Historic Places. It was from the rooftop of one of these buildings on the Las Vegas Plaza (now the Dice Apartments that face the plaza) that General Stephen Watts Kearney—in 1846—proclaimed New Mexico as a United States Territory.

After the arrival of the railroad in 1879, a new surge of prosperity flourished, attracting many fortune seekers and notorious characters to Las Vegas. The town became one of the wildest of the Wild West towns, playing host to the likes of Billy the Kid, Jesse James, Wyatt Earp, Bat Masterson, and Doc Holliday and his girlfriend, Big Nosed Kate. Before his move to Tombstone, Doc Holliday owned a gambling hall and saloon and a dental office in Las Vegas. At the turn of the century, Las Vegas became the largest town and one of the most important trading and financial centers in New Mexico.

Everything a visitor could wish to do and see is in and around Las Vegas. Summer or winter, the recreational opportunities are abundant: fishing, hunting, camping, water-skiing and windsurfing, sledding, ice skating, and cross-country skiing—all just minutes away. For overnighters, Las Vegas is a full-service town with good accommodations, gas stations, stores, and restaurants serving authentic Southwestern cuisine.

91

*Madison Vineyards
Winery and Tasting Room,
El Baranco, New Mexico.*

MADISON VINEYARDS

The Madison Vineyards and Winery is located twenty-five miles southwest of Las Vegas, New Mexico, alongside the Pecos River in the small village of El Barranco, just six miles north of the small village of Villanueva on NM 3. Bill and Elise Madison founded the winery in 1980. Bill noticed one plant behind the outhouse on their property and thought it was such a pretty plant that he decided to plant a vineyard there. So the vineyard began with some recommendations from Vince Rosingana, who owned the Santa Fe Vineyards north of Española, and from some suggestions offered by a wine writer, Richard Jones. Bill followed their advice on the kinds of grapes to grow. After some trial and error he started their vineyards with seventy vines. During the next three years, eighteen hundred vines were planted on two and a half acres. The vines consisted of French hybrids and vinifers. The winery began production in 1985 with a total output of three hundred gallons. The production has increased to between three and four thousand gallons annually, which includes award-winning dry and semi-sweet wines.

Because of the harsh winters and high water table, the quality and quantity of the yield depends on the weather conditions. Some years are more productive than others. The Madisons have gone through periods of crop failure due to heavy hailstorms and extreme temperature changes. Since the area is not an ideal place to grow grapes, Bill does not grow all of the grapes used in his wine production. He buys from growers in Dixon and from Santa Rosa, Albuquerque, and Belen. Bill does all of the physical work in the operation, but his wife, Elise, is the winemaker, and is blessed with a keen palate and excellent judgment—some of the requirements for great winemaking. They both acquired their experience from many wine tastings conducted by knowledgeable oenephiles, by asking questions, seeking advice, and learning through hands-on experimentation. Through these associations, Bill and Elise gleaned much knowledge about the subject of winemaking, its evaluation and science of production, and its types and merits.

The Madisons consider their Pecos Wildflower their signature wine. It is a smooth, fruity blend of the Muscat, a Riesling, and a Seyval. They make both dry red and dry white wines. Their Flyin' Saucer wine was released in 1997 to commemorate the fiftieth anniversary of the purported UFO crash north of Bill's former home in Roswell, New Mexico.

The Madison wines can be purchased in Albuquerque at Kelly Liquors, Jubilation Wines and Spirits, Quarters, Cost Plus, at Albertson's in Santa Fe, and some stores in Las Vegas. See the facing page for more information on its facilities and tasting room hours.

DIRECTIONS FROM ALBUQUERQUE:

From Albuquerque take I-40 east 72 miles to Clines Corners.
Continue east on I-40 another 15 miles to junction with
NM 3. Go north on NM 3 for about 20 miles to Villanueva,
and continue about 6 miles to the winery and vineyards.
It is on the left side of the road.

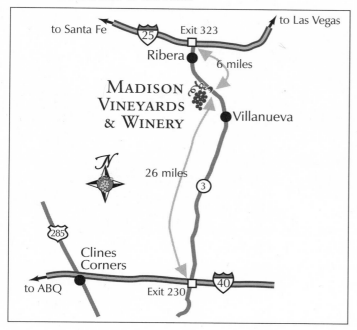

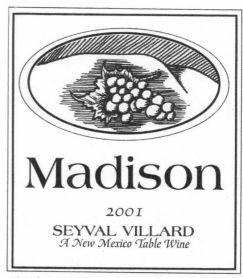

Vinted & Bottled by Madison Vineyards, NMBW #68
Ribera, New Mexico 87560

WINERY DETAILS:

Acres in Production: 2.5

Elevation: 6,391 feet

Hours: Mon.–Sat. 10 A.M.–5 P.M., Sun. noon–5 P.M.
(closed Wed.) Open Mar. 1–Jan. 31; Feb. by appt.

Proprietor: Bill and Elise Madison

Distance from Albuquerque: approximately 125 miles

Location: 6 miles north of Villanueva and about 25 miles
southwest of Las Vegas, New Mexico, off NM 3.

Mailing Address: HC 72, Box 490, Ribera, NM 87560

Telephone: (505) 421-8028

E-mail: madison@etsc.net or madison@plateautel.net

Founded: 1985

Grape Varietals: Baco Noir, Seyval Blanc, Sauvignon Blanc,
Muscat, Riesling

Wine Types: dry whites and reds, blends, and semi-sweets

Wine Procurement: Albertsons in Santa Fe, and in
Albuquerque at Kelly Liquors, Jubilation Wines & Spirits,
Cost Plus, and Quarters; and in some stores in Las Vegas

WINERY FACILITIES:

Tasting Room: Yes

Meeting Room: No

Picnic Site: No

Restrooms: No

Snacks: No

Lodgings: in Las Vegas

*For information on Glassware and
Tasting, Wine Service and Cooking
with Wine, and Wine Storage, see
appendix Wine ABCs beginning
on page 110.*

93

Camel Rock. Carved and eroded by wind and rain, Camel Rock is one of the most photographed sites in New Mexico. Fifteen miles south of Española off US 285.

94

Española

In the vicinity of Española are three wineries. They are Santa Fe Vineyards, Los Luceros Winery, and Black Mesa Winery.

Española is located in the beautiful Española Valley at an elevation of 5,595 feet above sea level. It has a population of 12,200. It is eighty-six miles north of Albuquerque and twenty-four miles northwest of Santa Fe. Its central location, between the Jemez Mountains (at 12,000 feet) to the west and the Truchas Peaks (at 13,000 feet) to the east, provides easy access to the spectacular and diverse recreation, historical areas, and archaeological sites of northern New Mexico.

Española was established in the 1880s as a stop on the Denver and Rio Grande Railroad. The town has grown to be the commercial center of the Española Valley. It once was the home of dinosaurs, whose remains are still being found near Abiquiu, just a few miles to the north. In 1855, Congress appropriated thirty thousand dollars to import almost one hundred camels to the Southwest territory. But the experiment was unsuccessful due to the lack of interest and acceptance of the strange animals' peculiarities. The tale is told that a weary camel stopped to rest next to Tesuque Pueblo and, too tired to move on, turned to stone. It is now called "Camel Rock" and stands on the west side of US 285, sculpted by wind and rain, and it is one of the most photographed sites in New Mexico. More than a thousand years ago, the Ancestral Puebloan Indians settled in this valley. Their ruins stand today in the cliff dwellings at Puye, just ten miles west of Española on NM 602. Their descendants still live in Santa Clara Pueblo, the location of the Puye dwellings, and in the other Indian pueblos scattered throughout the Española Valley.

In 1598, the Spanish led by Don Juan de Oñate settled near San Juan Pueblo. Five miles north of Española, across the river from San Juan Pueblo, a cross marks the site of the pueblo that the Spanish took over and established as the first capital of New Mexico. After the coming of the railroad in the 1880s, the three cultures of Indian, Spanish, and American blended. Their evidence and influences still pervade the Española Valley in the languages spoken, the religion, and the food. In Española, there are grocery stores, medical facilities, motels, and restaurants. Within an hour's drive from Española are perhaps the best hunting, fishing, boating, and skiing in New Mexico. Just a few miles north of Española off NM 68 are the wineries, vineyards, and tasting rooms of Black Mesa Winery, Los Luceros Winery, and Santa Fe Vineyards. About nine miles northeast of Velarde are La Chiripada Winery and Vivac Winery, which are both located in the small village of Dixon (see page 103).

95

*Santa Fe Vineyards,
Española, New Mexico.*

SANTA FE VINEYARDS

Santa Fe Vineyards is located twenty miles north of Santa Fe off US 285, sitting at an elevation of 6,000 feet above sea level. It was founded in 1982 by Leonard Rosingana (now deceased). Leonard came to New Mexico from Livermore, California, where he was the founder of Stoney Ridge Winery. He later moved to Santa Fe, taking his winemaking equipment with him, and established Santa Fe Vineyards. A skilled winemaker, Leonard's high standards of production have resulted in some of the finest wines produced in New Mexico—well known not only for their excellence, but also for their distinctive labels. Their original artwork was done by well-known artist Amado Peña, whose gallery is located at 235 Don Gaspar in Santa Fe. The Amado Peña Gallery is also the home of the Santa Fe Vineyards second tasting room and welcomes visitors.

Much of the winery's continued success since the passing of Leonard Rosingana is due to the management skills and dedication of its general manager, Dan Dougharty, who now oversees the entire operation, from bottling to corking to labeling. Years ago, Dan came to help his friends, Leonard and Donna Rosingana, for one season. His fascination resulted in Dan's resignation from corporate life and he is still there.

To insure the high quality of their wine production they do not grow their own grapes. They buy quality grapes from other grape growers to meet their high standards. They buy from Grand River Vineyards in Colorado, and some from the Gruet Vineyards in Truth or Consequences. Depending on the season's supply, they crush anywhere from fifteen to forty tons annually and produce seven to eight thousand cases per year. Their winemaker is Mark Matheson, who was trained at the University of California at Davis where he earned a winemaking degree. Mark has been with the company seven years.

Santa Fe Vineyards uses American oak barrels and mixed types of European barrels as well. The winery produces ten wines. They consider their Cabernets and a couple of good Chardonnays their signature wines. Their most unique wine is their Indian Market White, which is a blend of Muscat Canelli and Riesling. My personal favorite, which I store in my own wine cellar, is Tinto del Sol, a fine, smooth-tasting red table wine, which I feel can compete in quality with any good import. It is a house blend of Sauvignon Blanc, Semillon, and a French hybrid, Seyval.

For more details on Santa Fe Vineyards' visiting hours and facilities, see the facing page.

96

DIRECTIONS FROM ALBUQUERQUE:

Take I-25 north to Santa Fe. Take Exit 282, US 84/285, go through Santa Fe and head 20 miles north. Just off the highway is the winery, gift shop, picnic area, and tasting room of Santa Fe Vineyards. (Another tasting room is located in the Amado Peña Gallery at 235 Don Gaspar in downtown Santa Fe.)

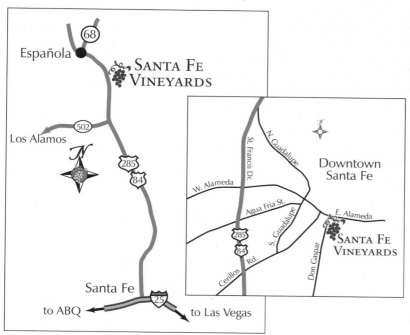

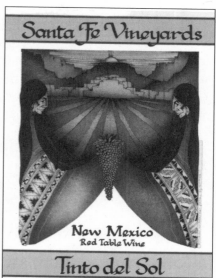

WINERY DETAILS:

Acres in Production: None, grapes are purchased

Elevation: 6,000 feet

Hours: Winery: Mon.–Sat. 10 A.M.–5 P.M., Sun. noon–5 P.M. Santa Fe Tasting Room: Mon.–Sat. 11 A.M.–5 P.M., Sun. noon–5 P.M.

Proprietor: the Rosingana family

Distance from Albuquerque: 80 miles

Location: 30 miles north of Santa Fe (on highway to Taos), 3 miles south of Española

Mailing Address: Route 1, Box 216A, Española, NM 87532

Telephone: Winery: Phone/Fax (505) 753-8100; Santa Fe Tasting Room: (505) 982-3477 or (800) 477-2571

Website: www.santafevineyards.com

Founded: 1982 by Leonard Rosingana (deceased)

Grape Varietals: Chardonnays, Cabernets, Muscat Canelli, Riesling, White Zinfandel

Wine Types: dry red and white table wines, dessert wines, and some blends

Wine Procurement: Smith's, Albertsons, Bird of Paradise, Quarters

WINERY FACILITIES:

Tasting Room: no appointment needed

Meeting Room: No

Picnic Site: outdoors with trees and tables

Restrooms: Yes

Snacks: No

Lodgings: in Española

For information on Glassware and Tasting, Wine Service and Cooking with Wine, and Wine Storage, see appendix Wine ABCs beginning on page 110.

97

Los Luceros Winery.
Photo by Bruce Noel.

LOS LUCEROS WINERY
(IN ALCALDE)

The Los Luceros Winery is owned and operated by Bruce and Sue Noel. They broke ground for their vineyard and winery in 1997. The winery is the second straw-bale winery building constructed in the country. It is located nine miles north of Española in one of the earliest viticultural sites in North America. More than four centuries ago (in 1598), Franciscan friars traveling with Don Juan de Oñate planted vines in the area to grow grapes for their sacramental wines.

Bruce is the chief winemaker. They have 1.1 acres in production, and depending on the variable weather conditions, they expect to average about three tons of grapes, which should yield about one hundred cases of wine. Bruce has been practicing the art of winemaking for about thirty years. He has no assistants. It is a hands-on operation dedicated to the production of the greatest wines from his grapes and other grapes purchased from growers in the area. Los Luceros vineyards produce Seyval Blanc, Vidal Blanc, Cayuga, Baco Noir, and some Chardonnay. To insure quality production, Bruce spares no expense, investing in French and American oak barrels for his super premium wines. They consider their signature wine their Baco Noir. Another popular wine is their Leon Noir. Their wines can be purchased at the winery and at festivals. Visitors to the tasting room are urged to call for an appointment to enjoy a great wine-tasting experience. For more detailed information on the winery's facilities and accommodations, see the facing page.

98

DIRECTIONS FROM ALBUQUERQUE:

Take I-25 north to Santa Fe. Take Exit 282, US 84/285, go through Santa Fe and head to Española. At Española take NM 68 and continue north to County Road 0048. Turn left and continue until CR 0048 ends at CR 1097. Turn left and follow signs to Los Luceros Winery on the right.

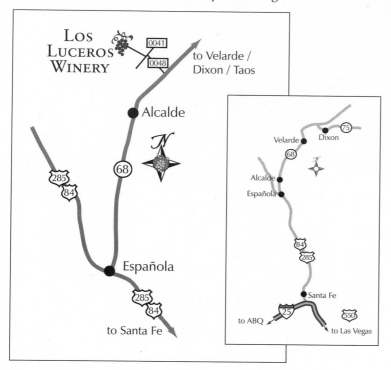

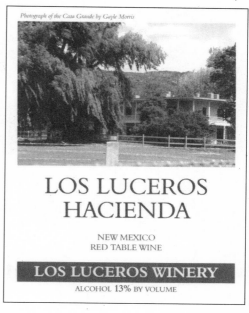

Photograph of the Casa Grande by Gayle Morris

LOS LUCEROS HACIENDA

NEW MEXICO
RED TABLE WINE

LOS LUCEROS WINERY

ALCOHOL 13% BY VOLUME

WINERY DETAILS:

Acres in Production: 1.1

Elevation: 5,700 feet

Hours: Weekends and holidays, noon–dusk.
Other times by appointment.

Proprietor: Bruce and Sue Noel

Distance from Albuquerque: 93 miles

Location: 9 miles north of Española

Mailing Address: PO Box 1100, Alcalde, NM 87511

Telephone: (505) 852-1085 or (505) 753-7925

Fax: (505) 753-6863

Founded: 1997

Grape Varietals: Seyval Blanc, Vidal Blanc, Cayuga

Wine Types: red and white table wines, Baco Noir
(Baco Noir Reserve is their premium wine)

Wine Procurement: at winery and festivals

WINERY FACILITIES:

Tasting Room: Yes

Meeting Room: No

Picnic Site: Yes

Restrooms: handicapped accessible

Snacks: No

Lodgings: In town of Española 9 miles south

For information on Glassware and Tasting, Wine Service and Cooking with Wine, and Wine Storage, see appendix Wine ABCs beginning on page 110.

For information on Glassware and Tasting, Wine Service and Cooking with Wine, and Wine Storage, see appendix Wine ABCs beginning on page 110.

99

*Black Mesa Winery,
Velarde, New Mexico.*

BLACK MESA WINERY
(IN VELARDE)

Gary and Connie Anderson founded the Black Mesa Winery in 1992. Jerry Burd and his wife, Lynda, purchased the winery in the year 2000. The winery is located in the small village of Velarde in the scenic Velarde Valley. It is situated in the ancient vineyards of early America at the mouth of the Rio Grande, off the historic Camino Real (the main highway between Santa Fe and Taos).

About seven or eight years before Jerry and Lynda purchased the Black Mesa Winery operation, Jerry was at a point where he wanted to change his direction in life. He was raised on a farm and wanted to grow grapes, realizing that many acres of grapes would afford him a profitable living. He decided to research, study, and learn the techniques of winemaking. Having accomplished this, he found and purchased the Black Mesa Winery. The Burds are now in their fourth year of operation with three and a half acres in production.

They grow about 20 percent of the grapes used in their wine. Their vineyard produces Syrah, Merlot, Riesling, Cabernet, and Chardonnay grapes. They purchase grapes from other growers, mostly from Deming, but also from Texas, Washington, Oregon, and Colorado. In 2002 they pressed fifty tons. One fun-filled weekend a year they press with their feet, providing fun for their neighbors who participate in the event—nothing formal, just a friendly group who stomp the grapes, drink wine, and picnic. In the year 2003 they produced three thousand cases.

Jerry is the chief winemaker and has a part-time assistant who holds a degree in chemistry. His main function is to assist in the chemistry and quality control of the wine production; another man assists in the labor. They use 50 percent French oak and 50 percent American oak barrels in the finishing process. All of their reds and some of their whites are finished in French oak, including Chardonnays, Cabernets, and a limited amount of Rieslings. They have two signature wines— Coyote, which is a dry Cabernet-Syrah blend excellent with hot, spicy foods, and Black Beauty, a red wine infused with chocolate. It is a dessert-type wine, not as sweet as a Sauterne, but it is a delight when consumed with a chocolate-based dessert. Black Mesa produces twenty other types of wine. For more information on wine procurement and the winery, see the facing page.

100

DIRECTIONS FROM ALBUQUERQUE:

Black Mesa Winery is located between Santa Fe and Taos on NM 68. Take I-25 north to Santa Fe. Take Exit 282, US 84/285, go through Santa Fe to Española. At Española take NM 68 north and follow the signs to the Black Mesa Winery. It is located at the mouth of the canyon.

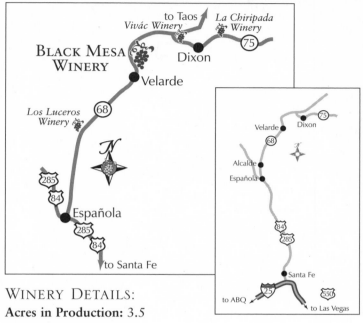

WINERY DETAILS:

Acres in Production: 3.5

Elevation: 5,600 feet

Hours: 10 A.M.–6 P.M. Mon.–Sat. year-round,
  Sunday noon–6 P.M.

Proprietor: Jerry and Lynda Burd

Distance from Albuquerque: 97 miles

Location: Velarde in northern New Mexico on NM 68,
  28 miles south of Taos, 15 miles north of Española

Mailing Address: 1502 Highway 68, PO Box 308,
  Velarde, NM 87582

Telephone: (505) 852-2820 or (800) 852-Mesa

E-mail: jer@blackmesawinery.com

Website: www.blackmesawinery.com

Founded: 1991 by Gary and Connie Anderson, transfer of
  ownership to Jerry and Lynda Burd in 2000

Grape Varietals: 26 in production including Chardonnay,
  Cabernet Sauvignon, Merlot, Cabernet Franc, and Riesling

Wine Types: table and blends

Wine Procurement: on-site and in Albuquerque at Quarters,
  Cost Plus, Kelly Liquors, Albertsons in Los Lunas,
  Raley's in Santa Fe, and the Liquor Barn in Taos

WINERY FACILITIES:

Tasting Room: Yes

Meeting Room: Yes

Picnic Site: Yes

Restrooms: Yes

Snacks: No

Lodgings: 5 miles away, just
  north of Española. Also in
  Santa Fe and in Taos.

For information on Glassware and Tasting, Wine Service and Cooking with Wine, and Wine Storage, see appendix Wine ABCs beginning on page 110.

101

↢ ESPAÑOLA

St. Anthony's Church, built in 1929, Dixon, New Mexico.

102

Dixon

There are two wineries in the vicinity of Dixon, La Chiripada Winery and Vivac Winery.

Dixon is a tiny village located alongside the Embudo River, two miles northeast of the junction of highways 68 and 75. It is a charming little town sitting at an elevation of 6,000 feet above sea level and nestled in the fertile Embudo Valley, dotted with farms and apple orchards amid a patchwork of artist studios, shops, century-old structures, and rustic homes that offer visitors a glimpse of an Hispanic past. It is also an artist community. During the first weekend in November it hosts the Annual Studio Tour. During this novel cooperative venture of the community, artists, jewelers, artisans, potters, and patrons of the arts conduct tours of the village studios, shops, and La Chiripada Winery and El Bosque Garlic Farm. This event is well worth a visit and is becoming more popular each year.

103

*La Chiripada Winery,
Dixon, New Mexico.*

LA CHIRIPADA
WINERY & VINEYARDS

La Chiripada is the oldest winery in northern New Mexico. It is located in the small village of Dixon, New Mexico, in the fertile Embudo Valley. It is a family-owned and operated winery, which was opened for business in 1981 by two brothers, Michael and Patrick Johnson. Michael, a former high school teacher, and Patrick, a professional potter, had a keen interest in winemaking. Both brothers took wine courses, researched winemaking and grape cultivation techniques, and gained much knowledge and experience in their early years of work in the vineyards of California.

In the late 1970s, they bought a tract of land in the fertile Embudo Valley. In 1977 they planted an experimental vineyard with one hundred French hybrids, which are cold tolerant and manage to survive in the harsh, freezing winter temperatures that occur in this valley. Michael and Patrick grow eight different varieties of French hybrids. They also grow Rieslings, which, like the French hybrids, ripen early in the short (four-and-a-half-month) growing season at this high altitude of 6,000 feet. Their Chardonnay grapes are purchased from growers in Deming and Truth or Consequences, from which they produce an excellent wine called Chardonelle, a blend of Chardonnay and Seyval Blanc.

La Chiripada Vineyards comprise eleven acres in production. Five of the eleven belong to the winery and the other six to a neighbor who is under a production contract with the Johnsons. They crush about sixty tons annually, which yields thirty-five hundred cases. The chief winemakers are Michael and Patrick. Patrick's oldest son, Joshua, works in the cellars and in the vineyard. The Johnsons' investment in Hungarian and American oak barrels to age their premium wines, their dedication to maintaining a goal of quality rather than quantity, and their method of doing everything by hand, including bottling and corking, has established La Chiripada as a leader in winemaking excellence. This dedication has rewarded them with a continuous string of award-winning wines and praise among prestigious wine reviewers, connoisseurs, and consumers.

La Chiripada considers their two signature wines the Rio Embudo White and the Rio Embudo Red. Both wines have earned gold medals. Their Rieslings are also award winners, best sellers, and the wine that they are best known for. La Chiripada wines range in style from dry, barrel-fermented whites to delightfully fruity, picnic-style wines, and cellar-quality reds. All of these excellent award-winning wines can be purchased at the winery in Dixon, tasting room on the Taos Plaza, Kelly Liquors and Quarters in Albuquerque, and the Liquor Barn in Santa Fe. For more information on La Chiripada's facilities and visiting hours please see the facing page.

104

DIRECTIONS FROM ALBUQUERQUE:

Take I-25 north to Santa Fe. Take Exit 282, US 84/285, go through Santa Fe to Española. In Española take NM 68 to junction of NM 75. Turn right (east) on NM 75 and go 3 miles to Dixon and follow signs to the winery.

WINERY DETAILS:

Acres in Production: 11

Elevation: 6,000 feet

Hours: Winery: Mon.–Sat. 10 A.M.–6 P.M., Sun. noon–6 P.M.
  Taos Plaza: Mon.–Sat. 11 A.M.–6 P.M., Sun. noon–6 P.M.

Proprietor: Patrick and Michael Johnson

Distance from Albuquerque: 109 miles

Location: 50 miles north of Santa Fe, 25 miles south of Taos

Mailing Address: PO Box 191, Dixon, NM 87527

Telephone: Dixon Phone/Fax: (505) 579-4437;
  Taos: (505) 751-1311 or (800) 528-7801

E-mail: info@lachiripada.com

Website: www.lachiripada.com

Founded: 1981

Grape Varietals: Chardonnay, Riesling, French hybrids

Wine Types: table wines, dry whites and reds

Wine Procurement: in Albuquerque at Jubilation, Kelly Liquors, and Quarters; in Santa Fe at the Liquor Barn, at the winery (junction of NM 68 and 75), and at the Taos Plaza tasting room

WINERY FACILITIES:

Tasting Room: Yes

Meeting Room: No

Picnic Site: room to picnic on lush lawns

Restrooms: Yes

Snacks: No

Lodgings: two bed and breakfasts in town

For information on Glassware and Tasting, Wine Service and Cooking with Wine, and Wine Storage, see appendix Wine ABCs beginning on page 110.

105

Vivac Winery Tasting Room,
junction of highways 68 and 75,
gateway to Dixon, New Mexico.

VIVAC WINERY

The Vivac Winery is one of the newest wineries in New Mexico. It is nestled in one of the most beautiful areas of northern New Mexico, alongside the Embudo River in the lush Embudo Valley in the small village of Dixon.

It is owned and operated by two brothers, Chris and Jesse Padberg, who planted the vineyard in 1998, received their license to sell wine in 2001, and opened for business in 2003. In 2002, they crushed about three tons of grapes that yielded about four hundred gallons.

According to Chris, the name Vivac is derived from *bivouac,* a term meaning "outpost" or "encampment" (or the last place you can get food or drink before heading into the mountains). In their case it relates to the last place you can grow grapes due to the high altitude. The vineyard consists of two acres with room to expand another six acres. The Padbergs grow Merlot, Foch, Pinot Noir, and Cayuga grapes. Cayuga produces a good white wine. They also purchase grapes from other New Mexico growers. The brothers purchase some from the Gruet Vineyards, and some from New Mexico Wineries, Inc., in Deming.

Jesse and Chris are the chief winemakers, whose experience and kills were developed through intensive research and study of the subject of oenology through extension courses from the University of California at Davis and by seeking and heeding advice from helpful, knowledgeable vintners like Pat and Mike Johnson, neighbors and owners of La Chiripada Winery, also located in Dixon.

Chris and Jesse use oak barrels for finishing their Chardonnays and their reds. They already are recognized as an up-and-coming, quality wine producer. Their wines can be purchased and sampled at their attractive tasting room located at the junction of NM 68 and 75 on the approach to the winery. For more detailed information on visiting hours and facilities, see the facing page.

106

DIRECTIONS FROM ALBUQUERQUE:

Take I-25 north to Santa Fe. Take Exit 282, US 84/285, go through Santa Fe to Española. In Española take NM 68. Continue north about 6 miles past Velarde till you come to the tasting room sign and building at the junction of NM 68 and NM 75.

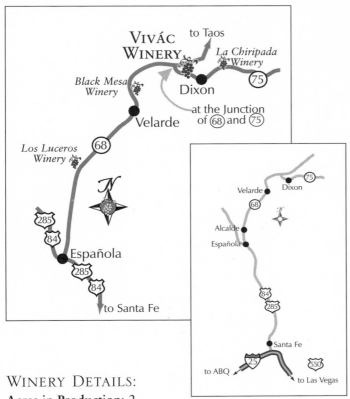

WINERY DETAILS:

Acres in Production: 2

Elevation: 6,200 feet

Hours: Mon.–Sat. 10 A.M.–6 P.M., Sun. noon–6 P.M.

Proprietor: Jesse and Chris Padberg

Distance from Albuquerque: 110 miles

Location: about 25 miles northeast of Española

Mailing Address: PO Box 234, Dixon, NM 87527

Telephone: (505) 579-4441

Fax: (505) 579-4575

E-mail: jesse@vivacwinery.com

Website: www.vivacwinery.com

Founded: 1998

Grape Varietals: Merlot, Baco Noir, Cabernet, Pinot Noir, Syrah, Cayuga

Wine Types: table, blends, and dessert

Wine Procurement: tasting room

WINERY FACILITIES:

Tasting Room: Yes

Meeting Room: No

Picnic Site: Yes

Restrooms: Yes

Snacks: No

Lodgings: in Española and Taos

For information on Glassware and Tasting, Wine Service and Cooking with Wine, and Wine Storage, see appendix Wine ABCs beginning on page 110.

107

APPENDICES

WINE ABCs

Grape Varietals

There are many varieties of grapes. Four of the most popular in wine production are Chardonnay, Cabernet Sauvignon, Merlot, and Zinfandel.

Chardonnay: Chardonnay is a great wine-producing grape and one of the most popular. It produces a high-quality white wine with a fruity aroma of apple and citrus. Often, a noticeable aroma of oak and vanilla, from contact with the oak barrel in which it is fermented, may be present. Good-quality Chardonnay has a balance of sweetness and tartness.

Cabernet Sauvignon (Cab-air-nay So-vee-nyon): These grapes are small and late-maturing, producing a delicately balanced red wine that requires five to six years to mature. The wine releases aromas of currants, blackberries, and blueberries. Sauvignon Blanc (So-vee-nyon Blawn) produces excellent medium- to full-bodied white wine also called Fumé Blanc (Foo-may Blawn). This wine is usually tart with herbal aromas.

Merlot (Mair-low): This is an early-maturing red grape famous for producing some of the greatest red wines of the Bordeaux district in France. It produces wines of high quality, comparable to those of Cabernet Sauvignon, but with a lower tannin content, which allows them to be drunk young (within two years of release). Merlots are moderately fruity and well balanced, with aromas of dark berries.

Zinfandel: Both red and white wines are produced from the Zinfandel grapes. They are vigorous growers with a high production yield per acre. High-quality whites are fruity in flavor with an aroma of strawberry or raspberry and a good balance of sweetness and tartness. The wine does not require prolonged aging in the winery and all whites should be drunk soon after release. The red Zinfandels have a detectable aroma of berries and raisins. When carefully tended during production it results in an excellent, full-bodied, dry wine with a moderately light tannic level.

Riesling (Rees-ling): This popular and fine white German grape produces excellent dry white wines, also called Johannesburg Riesling or White Riesling. The wine has a floral bouquet and a fruity aroma of apple, peach, citrus, and pineapple. It is light- to medium-bodied and dry. When the grapes are harvested late in the season during advanced ripeness, the resulting wines are sweet.

Pinot Noir (Peeno-Nwar): These are early ripening, moderately vigorous-growing grapes—the grape that produces the great Burgundies of France and the basic grape used in the making of champagne. The red wines made from Pinot Noir are usually dry, with a light level of tannins, and are of high quality. They have a fruity bouquet and an aroma of red berries, such as strawberries and cherries.

Chenin Blanc (Shay-nan Blawn): Chenin Blanc produces a fine, dry white wine. It is a generic variation of the Pinot Noir and often sold as White Pinot.

Gewurztraminer (Geh-vairtz-tra-meen-er): Gewurztraminer is a spicy grape. (*Gewurz* means "spicy" in German.) These grapes produce moderately dry to sweet wines with a fruity flavor.

Wine Types

There are three major wine types: table wines, fortified wines, and sparkling wines.

Table Wines: Table wines may be red, white, or pink (rosés). They may range from 10 to 14 percent alcohol by volume. These wines comprise all the wines that are usually consumed with meals. No brandy or other distilled spirits are added to these wines. When table wine's fermentation is complete, the wine is done.

Fortified Wines: Fortified wines are wines to which a certain amount of distilled spirits, such as brandy, is added either during or after fermentation. They usually contain about 20 percent alcohol by volume. Fortified wines may range from dry to sweet and may be red or white. Some of the most popular fortified wines are Sherry, Port, Muscatel, Madeira, and Marsala. The sweeter ones are usually drunk after the dessert. The dry fortified wines are drunk as an *apéritif* (before the meal to stimulate the appetite).

Sparkling Wine: Sparkling wines are actually made the same way as champagne and produced from the same grape varieties, among them, Pinot Noir or Pinot Chardonnay, Meslier, and Pinot Meunier. Under strict law, the name "champagne" can be legally applied only to the wine that is produced in the province of Champagne in France. The wines using the identical process and the same variety of grapes but produced elsewhere are called "sparkling wine." Sparkling wines are a careful blend of two or more of the aforementioned grapes that are processed through a second fermentation either in tanks or corked in the bottle with much of the carbon dioxide of fermentation still in the bottle. This process is called *Methode Champenoise.*

Sparkling wines go well with meals and are the universal favorite for toasting and celebrating gala occasions.

111

Glassware and Tasting

Sparkling and bright in liquid light
Does the wine our goblets gleam in,
With hue as red as the rosy bed
Which a bee would choose to dream in,
Then to-night, with hearts as light
To loves as gay and fleeting
As bubbles that swim on the beaker's brim
And break on the lips while meeting
　　—CHARLES FENNO HOFFMAN, 1806–1884

Of the five senses, sight, smell, and taste are the primary essentials in meaningful wine tasting. The basic principle of wine tasting is the comparison between wines, and the evaluation of the characteristics that set off the greatness of each one. Wine's appreciation and enjoyment begins with the eye. Wine is enjoyed because it looks good, smells good, and tastes good, and the glass that it is served in enhances these three sensations. The wine's appearance and color served in the proper glass provides clues to the wine's identity. The color of the wine is determined by the grape variety, and is also influenced by the age of the wine, the method of the vinification, the ripeness of the grape at the time of pressing, and the area of its cultivation. The shape of the glass, too, influences the wine's taste. Traditionally, certain glasses were used for certain wines, but present-day usage favors the "all-purpose" glass. The ideal all-purpose glass is a large, tulip-shaped, long-stemmed, thin-crystal glass, in-curved at the top, whose capacity is about eight ounces. This shape is large enough to swirl the wine, an essential in wine tasting.

When swirled, the wine is exposed to more oxygen, which magnifies the fumes of the esters and aldehydes of the alcohol that are released upon evaporation on the sides of the glass. The preferred glass for champagne or sparkling wine is the egg-shaped glass, while smaller glasses are favored for white wines, since their aromas are sharper.

TASTING WINE

Tasting wine is not complicated and no special science is required to enjoy the experience, but a little knowledge is helpful to contribute to its enjoyment.

There is a definite order one must follow for proper and meaningful wine tasting, but before we learn these steps in wine tasting, it is necessary to know the importance of three of our sensory organs—sight (the eye), smell (the nose), and taste (the tongue and palate)—in the art of tasting.

112

glass for Chardonnay/Zinfandel

glass for Sparkling wine/ Champagne

all purpose glass

1. Sight (the eye): One of the most important of the sensory organs for the professional wine taster is the eye, since the appearance and the color of the wine even in its most subtle shades can provide clues to the wine's identity. The color of wine is determined by the grape variety, and is also influenced by the region of the grape's cultivation, the stage of the grape's ripeness when harvested and pressed, its method of vinification, and the wine's age.

The dry light-bodied wines from cooler climates are usually lightest in color, ranging from a very light to pale yellow. Fuller-bodied sweeter wines from advanced stages of grape ripeness are deeper in shades of yellow to a deep gold, and youthful red wines are usually dark red to a purple hue. The brownish color of wine is the result of slow oxidation involved in the aging process. All of these colors provide the clues a professional taster heeds when discerning a wine's identity.

2. Smell (the nose): The act of sniffing the wine in the glass is an important step in wine tasting. When sniffed, the wine activates the nerve endings in the olfactory bulb, which detect the "bouquet" or fragrance that results from release of the molecules of esters and aldehydes from the alcohol as they are exposed to oxygen and evaporate inside the glass.

3. Taste (the tongue and palate): The tongue discerns the four basic tastes of sweetness, sourness, bitterness, and saltiness. All the other tastes are involved in the taste of smell. Sweetness is detected at the tip of the tongue. Sourness, or acidity, is detected on the sides of the tongue. Bitterness is detected on the back or the top of the tongue. Saltiness is felt at the front and the sides of the tongue.

THE PROPER STEPS TO FOLLOW IN WINE TASTING

1. Pour a little wine in the glass (about one-third to one-half full). This allows room for the wine to be swirled. Now raise the glass to the light and view it from the top. Compare the shades of color. Note how the reds go from deep ruby to a purple hue. Note how the whites range

113

from very light to pale yellow to deep gold. Is it brownish in color? If brown, it is an indication of over-oxidation; this is called maderization. Is the wine hazy or cloudy? If so, spoilage is indicated. If clear and brilliant in color it may be a visual introduction to the taste of a fine wine.

2. Swirl the wine in the glass. Swirling aerates the wine, allowing the fumes of the bouquet to emerge. This is the reason why only a small quantity of wine is poured into the glass; spillage is prevented and more oxygen is exposed to the wine to release the fumes of the bouquet.

3. Take a deep sniff of the wine in the glass. The fumes that are released are registered in the olfactory bulb and after many tastings of the same wine, the smell is recognized and the wine can be identified.

4. Sip the wine—although you may be tempted to swallow it, hold off until you take in some air through the wine, and let it roll around the tongue and to the back of the throat. Now swallow the wine. It should leave a lingering fragrance in your mouth, and the longer the fragrance lasts, the greater the wine.

5. An exchange of opinions after the tasting adds to the learning experience as faults and attributes of a wine may be brought to the attention of others who may not have noticed them during the tasting. (For most commonly used tasting terms, see the following.)

TASTING TERMS

acidity: Tartness produced by natural fruit acids; balance of acidity and sweetness indicates a good wine.

aroma: The scent emanating from the wine (helps to determine the grape it is made from).

astringency: A mouth-puckering sensation produced by tannin in the wine. Young wines are high in astringency.

body: The fullness of wine on the tongue. White wines are lighter, reds are heavier.

bouquet: The fragrance of wine determined by fermentation and aging.

character: The scent, taste, and appearance of a wine that distinguish it from others.

dry: Taste opposite of sweet, a result of wine containing less than 5 percent of residual sugar.

flat: A dull, lifeless wine.

flatness: A soft wine without much body.

legs: The outline of the wine clinging to the sides of the glass as the wine descends after swirling. Legs, also called "tears," indicate the alcohol's effect on the wine's viscosity: the greater the viscosity, the greater the alcohol, and the slower the wine descends.

musty: A moldy taste or smell.

nose: A term referring to the combination of grape aroma and bouquet of a wine.

114

Service and Cooking with Wine

SERVING WINE

While properly stored and in the bottle, wine remains dormant, but wine is a living, breathing thing and when uncorked it comes alive and starts to breathe. It absorbs oxygen from the air and this oxidation brings out its bouquet, improving its smoothness, body, and flavor. So to take advantage of this process, a bottle of red wine should be un-corked about one hour before serving to allow it time to improve its flavor. White wine is more delicate and should be served upon opening to prevent loss of its fragrance and freshness if exposed to air too long. A rule of thumb is to serve full-bodied red wines at room temperature and lighter reds (such as rosés) slightly chilled. White wines should be chilled for one to two hours in the refrigerator before serving. Champagnes or sparkling wines should be drunk when opened to prevent the bubbles from escaping before the wine is consumed. An opened bottle with leftover wine should be re-corked and refrigerated. It will keep for a couple of days to be enjoyed later.

It is not our purpose to set down hard and fast rules as to what wines should be served with specific dishes. In choosing a wine, the best rule is to follow your taste. It is a delightful experience to discover the harmonious combinations for oneself, but of course these discoveries depend upon good judgment.

You would not find the combination of hot chocolate and shrimp palatable, nor would you eat candy before a mouthful of steak. So with wine, certain rules of good judgment should be considered. A dry Burgundy or Claret will taste harsh after a sweet Sauterne. The same is true if a dry wine or white wine is served with sweet sauces. Vinegar and fine wines are unfriendly to each other, so do not be surprised if a fine wine does not come up to expectations if drunk in combination with vinegar dressings. A good rule is to serve the lighter wine before the fuller-bodied wine, the dryer wine before a sweet, but above all, let your taste be your guide.

SUGGESTIONS AT A GLANCE

Appetizers	Sherry
Soups	Sherry
White meat and seafood	Dry white or red wine
Red meat and game	Dry red
Cheese	Burgundy or Port
Dessert	Sweet wine
Nuts	Port

115

COOKING WITH WINE

Wine is a food rich in vitamins. It tenderizes some meats and enhances the flavor of foods it is cooked with. In cooking with wine, the same general pattern of choosing wine and food combinations is followed: i.e., choose a white wine for dishes served with white wine, a red wine for dishes served with red wine. Remember, the better the wine, the better the results! The following may serve as a general guide:

APPETIZERS

Canapés, hors d'oeuvres, spreads   Use Sherry, mix in enough to moisten.

SOUPS

Vegetable with beef or game base   Use sherry or dry red.
Vegetable with chicken   Use sherry or Madeira.
Add three to four tablespoons just before serving.

MAIN DISHES

Red meat or game and salads   Use dry red, sherry, or Madeira.
White meat, seafood, creoles, and cream sauces   Use dry white wine.

EGGS

Use dry white or red and flavor to taste.

DESSERTS

Use sweet wine.

COOKING PROCEDURE WHEN ABOVE IS:

Baked: *use 1/4–1 cup in pan*
Broiled: *baste with wine*
Boiled: *add while cooking*
Fried: *add to batter or marinade*

*Note: Champagne or sparkling wine can be consumed anytime
and are complementary with all foods whether with meals or in cooking.*

Wine Storage

Variations of heat and cold are detrimental to conservation of wine—a cool, dark place away from too much light is best for the proper storage of wine. A non-fluctuating temperature is also beneficial for proper wine storage at home.

In short, a wine should be kept in a quiet, dark, sheltered spot where the temperature is fairly cool and constant (ideally, about 50 degrees Fahrenheit), and where the bottles are not subject to unnecessary movement or shaking while "resting."

The bottles should be stored on their sides so that the cork will stay moist and expand, to prevent air from entering the bottle and causing oxidation, which can damage the taste and quality of the wine. Unfortunately, not everyone may have room for a wine cellar, which would be ideal for wine storage, but if there is a spare closet or space available that can be converted into a wine cellar, it would serve adequately as a storage area. The photo is of a "do-it-yourself" cellar in an otherwise wasted space under some steps leading to an upper story in my home. It has served me well these many years.

ANNUAL EVENTS

MEMORIAL DAY WINE AND CHILE WAR FESTIVAL

Last weekend in May at Las Cruces Southern New Mexico State Fairgrounds
Chile and salsa cookout competition, wine tasting, music, and arts & crafts.

MEMORIAL DAY SPRING FEST

At Balloon Fiesta Park in Albuquerque
Wine tasting, music, food, and arts & crafts.

FOURTH OF JULY SANTA FE WINE FESTIVAL

At Rancho de las Golondrinas in Santa Fe
*Wine tasting, food, music, arts & crafts, plus demonstrations of wool weaving,
bread baking, traditional crafts, and meet New Mexico winemakers.*

LABOR DAY NEW MEXICO WINE FESTIVAL

At Bernalillo the first weekend in September
*Music, food, wine tasting, arts & crafts,
and meet New Mexico winemakers.*

HARVEST FESTIVAL LAS CRUCES

At the Southern New Mexico Fairgrounds
Wine tasting, food, and music.

NOTE:

*For information on dates and particulars call the
New Mexico Wine Growers Association or the
Vine & Wine Society (see next page for contact info).*

WINE ASSOCIATIONS

NEW MEXICO WINE GROWERS ASSOCIATION
380 Petaca Road
Ponderosa, NM 87044
Phone: (866) 4WINENM
Website: www.nmwine.net

VINE & WINE SOCIETY
PO Box 26751
Albuquerque, NM 87125
Website: www.vineandwine.org

GLOSSARY

Appellation d'Origine: Term on French wine labels signifying origin and legal right to the name it bears.

bouquet: Collection of fragrances the wine gives off.

cask: Large, wooden container for wines. Also called barrels.

chaptalization: The process of adding sugar to the musk (the fermenting wine).

climat: Another name for vineyard.

coupage: The blending of wine from various vineyards to get a better and more uniform quality.

cru: Vineyard or growth.

green: A wine too young to drink.

hard: A young wine, not fully matured.

hybrid: A grape that is propagated from a seed that is a cross of two varieties. Hybrids were developed to improve quality and withstand harsh climates. Developed in Europe to overcome the phylloxera disease that devastated the vines in the 1880s.

growth: A vineyard or the French *cru.*

maderized: A sweet wine that has darkened.

oenology (also spelled "enology"): Science or study of wine.

ordinaire: The common wine of everyday use in France.

Pourriture Noble (Translation: "noble rot"): A mold, scientifically called *Botrytis cinera*, which sets in after over-ripeness. (The stage grapes are picked in the Sauternes district of France, resulting in a very sweet dessert type wine.)

Rosé: A pinkish or pale red wine made by removal of the grape skins when desired shade of color is reached.

sec: French term for "dry."

tannin: The acid in wine that preserves its keeping quality.

tonneau: Equivalent to four barrels or ninety-six cases.

viniculture: Cultivation of grape-producing vines.

vintage: Date or year grapes were harvested and wine was made.

INDICES

INDEX
OF VICINITIES

All roads in vicinities below are paved.

VICINITY	ZONE	ROUTE AND ACCESSIBILITY
Alamogordo / Tularosa, 43	1, Southern	58 miles south of Carrizozo off US 84
Albuquerque, 55	2, Central	At intersection of I-25 and I-40
Anthony / La Union, 29	1, Southern	28 miles south of Las Cruces off NM 28
Belen / Bosque, 11	1, Southern	34 miles south of Albuquerque off I-25
Bernalillo / Placitas, 71	2, Central	At intersection of NM 44 and I-25
Bloomfield / Blanco, 79	3, Northern	At intersection of NM 44 and US 64
Corrales, 65	2, Central	4 miles northwest of Albuquerque
Deming, 33	1, Southern	53 miles west of Las Cruces off I-10
Dixon, 103	3, Northern	50 miles north of Santa Fe, 25 miles south of Taos off NM 580
Española, 95	3, Northern	25 miles north of Santa Fe via US 285
Las Cruces / Mesilla, 21	1, Southern	45 miles north of El Paso via I-10 and off I-25
Las Vegas / Villanueva, 91	3, Northern	25 miles south of Las Vegas via I-25
Los Alamos / White Rock, 87	3, Northern	18 miles south of Española off NM 502
Ruidoso, 39	1, Southern	41 miles south of Carrizozo via NM 37 and NM 38
San Ysidro / Jemez Springs, 83	3, Northern	23 miles northwest of Bernalillo off NM 44
Truth or Consequences, 15	1, Southern	149 miles south of Albuquerque off I-25

122

INDEX
OF WINERIES

123

INDEX
OF WINERIES

(continued)

All roads to vicinities below are paved.

WINERIES	ZONE	VICINITY
Sandia Shadows Vineyards & Winery, 18	1, Southern	T or C / Engle
Santa Fe Vineyards, 96	3, Northern	Española
Santa Rita Cellars (NM Wineries), 26	1, Southern	Las Cruces / Mesilla
Sisneros-Torres Winery, 12	2, Southern	Belen / Bosque
St. Clair Winery (NM Wineries), 34	1, Southern	Deming
Tularosa Vineyards, 44	1, Southern	Tularosa
Vivac Winery, 106	3, Northern	Dixon
Willmon Vineyards, 40	1, Southern	Ruidoso
Wines of the San Juan, 80	3, Northern	Bloomfield / Blanco

124

INDEX
OF LABELS

125